TOTAL QUALITY MARTIAL ARTS

TOTAL
Pathways to
QUALITY
Continuous
MARTIAL
Improvement
ARTS

CHRISTOPHER D. HESS, SMAC

MULTI-MEDIA BOOKS
Los Angeles • New York City

Disclaimer
Please note that the author and publisher of this book are NOT RESPONSIBLE *in any manner whatsoever for any injury that may result from practicing the techniques and/or following the instructions given within. Since the physical activities described herein may be too strenuous in nature for some readers to engage in safely, it is essential that a physician be consulted prior to training.*

Library of Congress Catalog Number: 98-68618
ISBN: 1-892515-03-2

First published in 1999 by
MULTI-MEDIA BOOKS,
a division of Multi-Media Communications Network, Inc.
Copyright © 1999 by Multi-Media Communications Network, Inc.
All rights reserved. No part of this publication may be reproduced or utilized in any form or by any means, electronic or mechanical, including photocopying, recording, or by any information storage and retrieval system, without prior written permission from Multi-Media Books.

Library of Congress Cataloging-in-Publication Data
Hess, Christopher D., 1960–
    Total Quality Martial Arts / by Christopher D. Hess.

DISTRIBUTED BY
Unique Publications
4201 Vanowen Place
Burbank, CA 91505
(800) 332–3330

First edition
05 04 03 02 01 00 99 98 97   1 3 5 7 9 10 8 6 4 2
Printed in the United States of America
Cover photographs by Hannah B. Hess
Text photographs by Dennis Gage, Wayne Kaiser, Hannah B. Hess, and Christopher D. Hess
Design by Kathryn Sky-Peck
Edited by: Mark V. Wiley

Gratitude

To Sensei Mark Long, for introducing me to "The Way" and allowing me to be myself.

To Tom Ehrhard, for his selfless introduction and willingness to nurture my curiosity in sport science training.

To Douglas Jeffrey, for providing my first chance and being a responsive editor.

To Mark Wiley, for believing, supporting, and bringing this work to publication.

To Marian and Hannah, for rounding out my edges.

TABLE OF CONTENTS

Gratitude v
Introduction ix

PART ONE: PHYSICAL CONSIDERATIONS 1

Introduction 3
Chapter One: Sport Science for Martial Athletes 7
Chapter Two: Creating the Annual Training Plan 25
Chapter Three: Strength and Nutrition Matters 49
Chapter Four: The Total Quality Performance Log 69

PART TWO: SPIRITUAL COMPONENTS 83

Introduction 85
Chapter Five: Assessing Potential 91
Chapter Six: Vocation 107
Chapter Seven: Relationships 121

PART THREE: CREATING OUR FUTURE 137

Introduction 139
Chapter Eight: For Ourselves as Martial Athletes: The Portfolio .141
Chapter Nine: For the Community of Martial Athletes:
    Choosing to Flourish or Survive .159

Chapter Ten: In the Eye of the Public:
    Enhancing Our Perception 179
Chapter Eleven: Why Martial Arts are the Best Exercise 191
Closing Thoughts 203
References 205
Appendix 212
Index 213
Photo Credits 216

INTRODUCTION

*"None of the secrets of success
will work unless you do."*
—PETE PEARSON

The ability to be number one is not available to everyone. But everyone has the same opportunity to continuously improve themselves and reach their individual potential. In many instances, life has demonstrated that an individualized sense of improvement and realization of potential is more satisfying than becoming a "champion." Perhaps that's the meaning behind Gandhi's statement that "satisfaction lies in the effort, not the attainment."

A large percentage of the martial arts community consists of people who want to be their very best. During the past five years, I've developed and used an approach that has enabled me and others to become their best. I call this approach Total Quality Martial Arts.

It is based on the Japanese practice of Total Quality Management (TQM), a concept I'll explain shortly. I've adapted the concepts of TQM to create a framework of continuous improvement for both the physical and spiritual dimensions of life. And spiritual includes aligning work and relationship responsibilities as well as the physical aspects of martial art practice.

The reason I am writing about this approach is because too many martial artists concentrate only on developing themselves physically, to excel at competition or self-defense. Without personal alignment in other matters of life, those who concentrate solely on the physical dimensions may be unable to address the demands of work, relationships, and personal choice.

It may not show up in the physical techniques of a given combat style, but misalignment in the physical and spiritual dimensions lurk in hearts and personal character and shows up in ways that undermine otherwise good intentions. And, even among those who exclusively emphasize the physical aspects of training, I've found many who are unable to properly train themselves to reach their potential. The overwhelming tendency in the martial arts community is to copy the program of a "champion" or "master" even though that program may not be based on accepted sport science for martial artists.

I invite you to use Total Quality Martial Arts to fulfill all that your life has to offer. The approach applies to anyone who wants to reach their maximum potential, regardless of the martial art system. It applies to anyone who recognizes that there is work to be done to fulfill their lives physically or spiritually. Theodore Roszak has stated that "we grow sick with the guilt of having lived below our authentic level." Total Quality Martial Arts is an alternative to that despair. Let me tell you how it began with me.

Total Quality Management

The TQM concept has been one of the most profound in business and industry over the past couple decades. TQM was originally created by a British scientist, R.A. Fisher,[1] who used basic scientific principles such as research, analysis and measurement in the field of agriculture to grow better crops. This was his system to reach maximum potential. These tenets were later modified and applied by American physicist Walter Shewhart for AT&T. While the early origins of this practice traveled from Britain to the United States, the first economy to actually adopt Total Quality practices in business and industry was Japan. They adopted this in their post World War II efforts to rebuild their economy, under the direction of Edward Deming and William Juran.

As a result of Japan's adopted use of Total Quality principles and successes in manufacturing, the concept was reintroduced to the United States by Lockheed aircraft in 1970. Along with the three core aspects of research, analysis, and measurement came another important concept adorned in Japanese meaning: *kaizen,* meaning continuous improvement.

Total Quality and the Martial Arts

You may be wondering how this successful business and manufacturing principle applies to the martial arts; why I've linked the two as a name for my approach. Let me give you an analogy. Although the origin of TQM is in agriculture, the practice has been most clearly applied to the manufacturing process. Picture for a moment a business that makes boats.

If you were in charge of this boat business and using TQM, you would do three fundamental things. First you would gather data about the best materials to use in the manufacturing process. Next, you would begin to manufacture boats and analyze how well these materials worked, both on the "conveyer belt" and in the water. Finally, you would use measure the quality of your boats by customer satisfaction standards, such as how many were returned to correct manufacturing errors.

TQM, of course, is much more complex than this and the basic example just cited can generate whole books of criteria to use in any of the three fundamental core principles. But as an analogy, it demonstrates how TQM can be applied to a martial artists.

I was first introduced to TQM in 1991 and quickly realized that its framework could be applied to contexts beyond business and industry. I used it to improve all categories of my life, including those that normally resist analysis. By using TQM, I can empirically demonstrate improvements in a physical and spiritual sense.

As a martial artist, you need a "whole life" approach to reach your potential. For instance, you should gather sport science research about human performance. This leads to creating an intelligent training plan, based on the sport science you study. Then, as you perform the plan, you should carefully record what you actually do and your reaction to it (weight gain or loss, strength changes, etc.). As in the boat example that illustrated TQM, you would measure the effectiveness of your training by comparing what you intend (the plan) versus what you realized (your actual performance).

The majority of U.S. martial artists are ages 7–16.

Sounds pretty easy, doesn't it? But hardly anyone, least of all martial athletes, do this. Numerous martial athletes try to adopt "winning formulas" from successful "stars" instead of using an approach that incorporates sport science and analyzes performance to reach individual potential. Too many use the techniques of others without understanding the underlying muscle and enzyme systems involved.

If the reigning champion of some sport consumes raw eggs each morning, we well-meaning, committed athletes are tempted to do the same (remember Rocky?). If another claims that running 10 miles a days guarantees success, we are tempted to emulate this example and often incur injury or overtrain in an effort to mimic another athlete's training plan. These efforts are usually made without any understanding of physiology or consideration of the previous level of individual training. Furthermore, almost without exception, these techniques are viewed in a vacuum; we may look at ways to achieve bigger biceps but don't consider how the other systems of our lives must be aligned to make this happen. For instance, alignment considers how our vocational and interpersonal systems must support the endeavor to create bigger biceps. Often, short-term success or outright failure is the "reward" in our one-dimensional pursuit of a short-term goal.

We have a special obligation to understand just what it means to align the systems of life and achieve "potential," since the majority of the estimated four million U.S. martial athletes are not adults.[2] It's a matter of social responsibility to teach our youth sound principles of training and how to flourish as human beings—how to be martial artists in the broadest sense.

To meet your physical ambitions, I will share with you a system for fulfilling your own potential that is based on an understanding of sport science and your performance. Instead of merely adopting the newest training methods offered in the most recent magazines, I'll share a system that enables you to determine your inherent potential and the means to achieve it. The Total Quality Martial Arts approach will enable you to gather data about yourself, analyze it, measure your progress, and find continuous improvement in the martial arts. You'll be able to help others as well.

About Myself

During the past two decades I have primarily practiced shotokan karate and taekwondo but have also studied and researched tai chi, aikido, and jeet kune do. In 1996, I became the first certified Specialist in Martial Arts Conditioning (SMAC) through the International Sport Sciences Association (ISSA). I am also a member of the National Strength and Conditioning Association (NSCA). I also received extensive training and certification as a licensed coach with the United States Cycling Federation (USCF), the organization that first introduced me to sport science.

Through the exceptional instruction offered by these organizations, I have learned how to apply sport science to martial athletes. I have used this learning to publish articles in magazines such as *Black Belt, Karate International, MA Training, Inside Karate, Karate/KungFu Illustrated,* and *Wushu KungFu.* I'm currently a columnist for *Martial Arts Illustrated.* But I offer even more than martial art experience, certification, and published articles to the important subjects addressed in this book. I also possess a masters degree in marketing

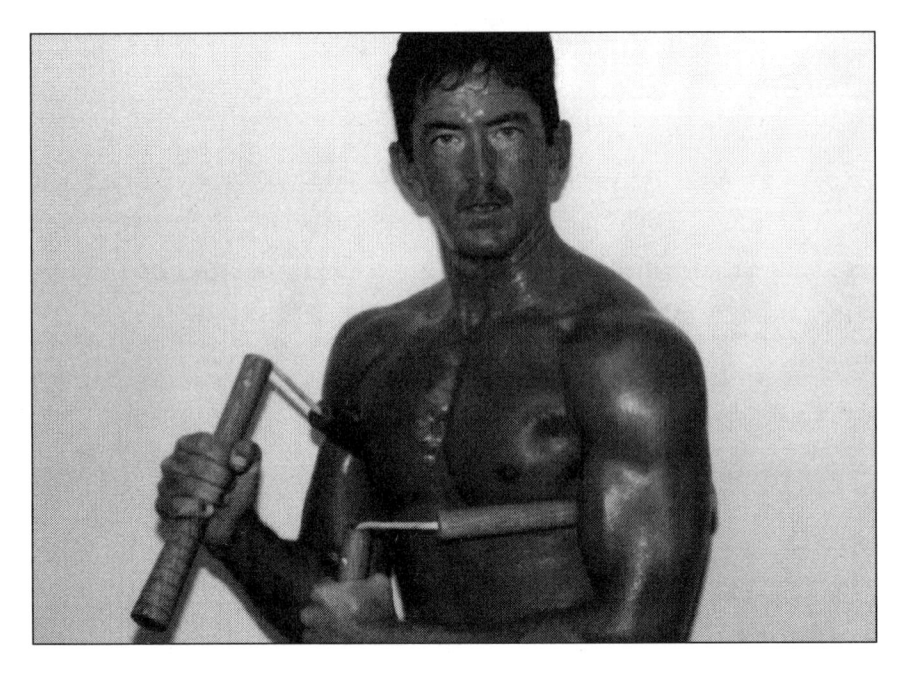

The author has effectively used these Total Quality principles in the martial arts . . .

with a special emphasis in the martial arts and I am a Master Facilitator of Total Quality Management.

It has been said that to write the truth, you must first become the truth. I have lived the principles outlined in this book and know, beyond a shadow of a doubt, that they are universal principles able to improve your life and athletic performance.

As an example of their effectiveness in the physical realm, I used these principles to help an average group of bicycle racers finish in the top three positions in 87% of the races we entered as a team. The "sport science" principles outlined in the first section of this book will help you understand which training principles to adopt and which ones to ignore. Other principles are experience-based, such as my use of TQM, and will help you analyze past training and plan your future training—based on sound sport science.

Equally significant is that I offer a fresh perspective on the spiritual aspects of martial arts. As discussed in section two, "spiritual" is not necessarily religious and neither is it some esoteric experience only reserved for the "enlightened." True spirituality involves your whole life: martial art practice, work, and relationships. Like the sport science, I have lived these attendant principles as well. After 15 years of marriage and recognition as a top performer in my career, I have learned much about interpersonal relationships and how these realms must support martial athletics.

This book is not about techniques, in the sense of choke-holds or other "how to" types of instruction. There are approximately 1,300 book titles on those subjects. I won't duplicate those works. Instead, this book is about identifying approaches needed to successfully perform those techniques. This approach can be applied to all martial athletes whether the system is "soft" or "hard," "internal" or "external." Since my own background is primarily in the striking arts of shotokan and taekwondo, many of the examples and references will be in that context. Please understand, however, that the physical emphasis in this book is about conditioning, and those principles apply to the training of any martial athlete.

Most of us want to be good athletes and human beings. Some want to be

. . . and as a competitive bicycle racer and coach.

the best. Our temptation is to rush out and read how a top competitor trains and to copy that program. But as I'll demonstrate, many top competitors are technically underachieving. That's right, underachieving—even as national champions.

Some of the concepts discussed herein will be new to you and may not feel as familiar as "run 10 miles" or "spar until you drop." However, if we as martial athletes are to become a learning community, we must carefully examine the fundamental principles of performance and potential.

To paraphrase Plato, you don't necessarily want to be the first to grab hold of the new, but you certainly don't want to be the last to let go of the old. Let's look at the Total Quality Martial Arts approach and begin our personal improvements right now. We'll look at the sport science, not just learning a certain system's techniques. We'll use Total Quality!

PART ONE

Physical Considerations

INTRODUCTION

"Be aware that a halo has to fall only a few inches to be a noose."
—DAN MCKINNON

You have no doubt watched that moment of exhilaration among combat athletes. Following a grueling contest with a world title at stake, the champion holds his or her belt above their heads in the victory salute. On the surface, this merely appears as a moment of pure joy and recognition of hard work, skill, and commitment. But at another level, these moments set certain cultures in motion.

After the belt is lowered and the victor steps back into daily life, people who have viewed the event naturally believe that the victor has "proof positive" training methods. A spectator naturally assumes that the earned success of those who train in combat sports such as martial arts, wrestling, or boxing justifies the training methods used. In other words, if these training methods helped "create a champion" then they should be used by others as well.

Unfortunately, this is not necessarily true. Some people are successful in competition despite training methods that, upon closer examination, have actually hindered realization of their full potential. As an example, combat athletes frequently misunderstand the role of aerobic capacity in their training. Our culture expresses a tenet that combat athletes should develop endurance with, perhaps, five mile runs to develop it.

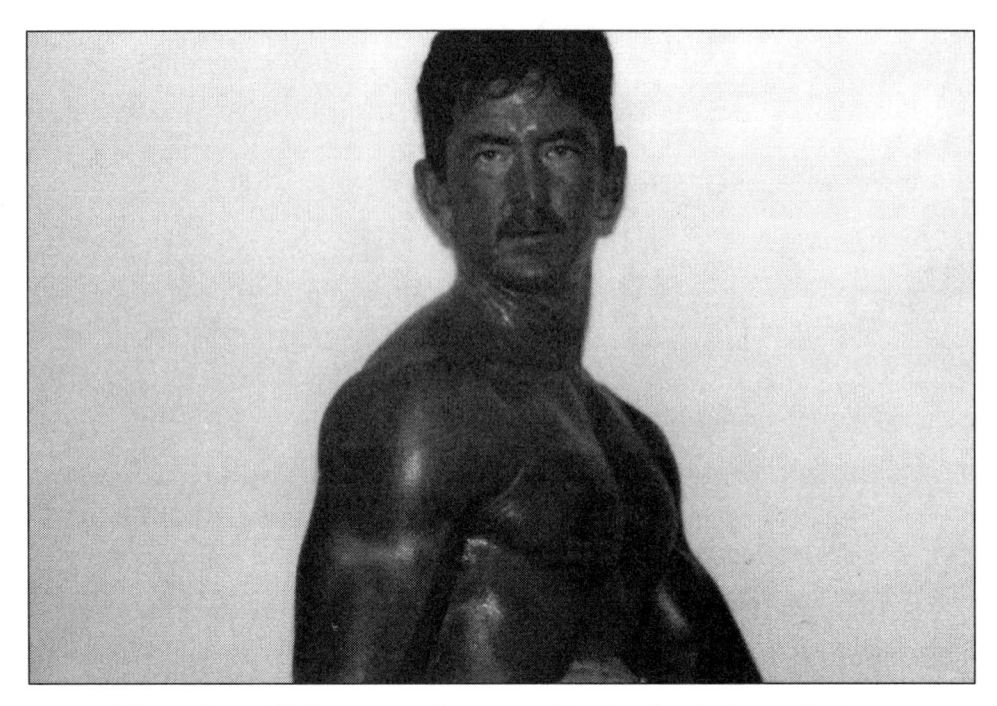

The author will demonstrate how to combine hard training and science.

Combat athletes who practice five mile runs are often unaware that reduced intensity aerobic activities recruit and train low-intensity muscle fibers and enzymes which undermine development of the high energy systems that combat athletes desperately want to develop.

Equally poignant is our training culture's misinterpretation of the "out of breath" signal. Somehow, many of us have been led to believe that if we become short of breath while engaged in high-intensity combat sport activity, it means we're not quite fit and probably need some aerobic activity to compensate our fitness. And yet, we have watched world class sprinters bend over and gasp for air after running 100 meters in less than 10 seconds without getting the connection: being fit doesn't mean we won't hurt or become winded. Being (combat) fir means we're able to do the task. Becoming winded may be no more than a sign of high intensity exertion.

To understand what it means to be fit and successful as a combat athlete requires an appreciation of the unique muscle fiber types and enzyme systems used in explosive, short-duration activities. With this in mind, in this section I review the fundamental sport science considerations inherent to martial art activity. This will enable you to train as smart as possible and take the next steps in realizing your physical potential.

That world title belt is a halo that implicitly endorses training methods and establishes cultures. However, success gained by methods that don't reflect sound sport science may become a noose when those who understand and adopt proven science train hard *and* smart. You have an opportunity to flourish through the training science presented in the next four chapters.

CHAPTER ONE

SPORT SCIENCE FOR MARTIAL ATHLETES

"The purpose of today's training is to defeat yesterday's understanding."
—MIYAMOTO MUSHASHI

All athletes are not created equal. Well-meaning people, including sports coaches and martial athlete instructors, have used the Declaration of Independence's maxim that "all men are created equal" to state that we can become whatever we want to as athletes. This is simply not true, at least as it relates to competition. Due in large part to certain inherited characteristics, such as body type, muscle fiber composition, and mental temperament, we cannot all become the next great martial athlete (relative to others). Instead, what we all equally have a chance to do is reach our potential, even overachieve it to a certain extent. How is it possible to overachieve potential, you ask? The following is an example.

In terms of lung capacity there are certain predicted values based on age, weight, and various other characteristics. At my last assessment, I have overachieved my predicted potential by 18% in scoring a value of 118% lung capacity. But even at that overachieved (well-trained) state, I do not measure up to a more gifted athlete who may outperform me while only at 90% of his or her potential. You see, we're not all created equal—but we all have an equal chance to maximize our individual potential. Expressed differently, I may run a 6:00 minute mile at my very best. A more (genetically) talented, but less trained athlete, may run a 5:30 mile. The difference is in potential as expressed in body type, muscle fibers, and mental temperament.

The steps we take to realize or even over-achieve our individual potential is, therefore, at the heart of our training. By adopting the Total Quality Martial Arts approach to our training process, we can determine our approximate potential and move toward realizing it.

The Stars

Have you read how your favorite martial artist trains? In the past, I've read (who knows if it's true?) that Jean-Claude Van Damme exercises on the stairmaster for one hour, three times per week. Or have you heard that Don Wilson runs five miles per day? That Chuck Norris spars for one hour every day?

Or perhaps you've read the (spartan) training regime that some reigning champion uses, whether in martial athletics, boxing, or wrestling. Since the person you're reading about is a champion, then the training methods he uses must be effective, right? Wrong!

Success does not justify training methods. Some people are successful in the ring despite their training methods. In many cases, conditioning drills and techniques are used that do not specifically develop the energy systems or muscle fibers needed for maximum performance. But the fact that these people are successful, despite themselves, obscures the issue and creates training myths that are difficult for coaches and trainers to dismantle. For years, superstar basketball player Michael Jordan refused to perform strength training and yet was successful. Was he right to ignore it? In 1996 he stated that he should have been doing it all along. Did Jordan's previous success justify his (inadequate) training methods? No it did not. Thus, we as martial athletes should not mistake success with realizing potential either.

To be like Bruce Lee requires studying sport science just as Lee did.

It is often hard to separate fact from fiction. Whether statements like those attributed to Van Damme, Wilson, or Norris are true or not, you'll see claims like these and be tempted to begin using those training programs right away. What looks good on the silver screen is easily imaginable in our minds. But martial sport science research is necessary to meet our goals. Superior athletes and trainers like Bill Wallace or Bruce Lee have not just blindly adopted someone's training routine. They researched and read. Wallace, in fact, has a masters degree in kinesiology.

So let's assume for a moment that Van Damme does exercise for one hour on the stairmaster three times per week. He looks good doesn't he? If it's true and he's good should you adopt that training program? Does his success justify the training method? Not necessarily. It depends on numerous variables. Does it train the muscles and energy systems that are part of your own set of goals (or his)? Is it within the range of exercise that you're currently performing (if you're doing no aerobic work now, too much too soon could lead to overtraining). Do you have the same amount of time to train as does a professional athlete or actor?

These are just a few of the questions that you must ask yourself before you can use the training methods of the stars. If Van Damme wants to have the fastest kicks possible and he's doing an hour of stairmaster work, then he's technically underachieving his goal. The same would apply to you if fast kicks are your goal. The reason for this "underachieving" is because of the energy systems and muscle development involved in delivering fast kicks and competing in "explosive" sports. In order to intelligently decide which training methods to use, you must understand these systems to succeed as a martial athlete. As the first step in the Total Quality Martial Art process, we must therefore conduct research about sport science.

Training Myth

What stands between you and an intelligent decision about training methods is what I previously referred to as the "training myth." For example, a myth exists concerning the relationship of running and success in either point karate or kickboxing. According to this myth, one should run as much as possible. If one is currently running five miles and yet becoming "winded" during sparring, then one should run 10 miles.

While this reasoning has a certain intuitive logic to it, it is incorrect according to sport science. In reality, the ability to perform successfully during intense bouts of two to three minutes in duration may be compromised or blunted by certain types of endurance training.[1] If some champion is running 10 miles a day and cites that as "proof positive" of success, sport science states that that champion could be even better if some of the (excessive) endurance training was reinvested into a better activity, like plyometrics. Success itself is not an adequate basis for intelligent training decisions.

The ability to perform successfully during intense bouts of two to three minutes in duration may be compromised by certain types of endurance training.

The reason for this seeming anomaly is that there are distinct types of energy systems and muscle fibers used for different types of athletic performance.

In order to be a (more) successful martial artist, these systems must be trained correctly. Let's examine each of them and then look at how they all fit together to create maximum performance relative to your individual goal.

Energy Systems

There are three energy systems that exist in the human body, although they are frequently summarized as five due to some functional overlap. Generally speaking, the three core systems are the phosphagen, glycolytic, and oxidative energy systems.

The phosphagen energy system is the one that supplies short-term, high intensity effort (a front snap kick). Physical efforts that use this energy last from zero to six seconds in length. In contrast to the other energy systems that will be described, phosphagen describes stored energy within the muscles and cells. Stored energy means that your exertion is not dependent on either oxygen or calories derived from carbohydrates or fats.

The phosphagen system supplies energy for high intensity efforts.

In application, a burst or flurry of kicks and/or punches that are performed in six seconds or less are using this stored energy of the phosphagen system. While the volume of this energy system is genetically small, it can be trained. With systematic training (to be explained shortly), the concentration of enzymes and intramuscular stores of adenosine triphosphate (ATP-PC) can be increased to store a larger capacity of energy. It must be emphasized, however, that this capacity (while powerful), is very small in duration compared to the other energy systems.

The glycolytic energy system is not as distinct as the other two systems. According to the level of intensity, the glycolytic system is either its own independent energy system or it interacts with the phosphagen or oxidative system to supply energy.

To further describe this phenomenon, the following chart illustrates the energy systems as they relate to the duration of effort:

TIME	ENERGY SYSTEM
0 to 6 sec.	Phosphagen
6 to 30 sec.	Phosphagen and Glycolytic
30 sec. to 2 min.	Glycolytic
2 to 3 min.	Glycolytic and Oxidative
Above 3 min.	Oxidative

Whereas the phosphagen system uses stored energy, the glycolytic system is an energy-producing system deriving from carbohydrate sources in the body. The process of glycolysis is frequently referred to as the "lactic acid" system.

The oxidative, or aerobic system describes those activities that are longer than three minutes in duration. The fuel for this energy system is stored fat in the body.

Application of Energy System Knowledge

As a martial athlete, you will use the energy system that meets the demand of your activity, which is primarily anaerobic.[2] Thus, if you are a point-fighter, you must focus on the primary energy needs of that activity (phosphagen or stored energy). For kickboxing, you would develop both the phosphagen and glycolytic energy systems.

The specific targeting and development of these systems is of paramount importance. Aerobic training that exceeds your (high energy) martial arts goals will compromise or blunt success. This is because extended aerobic training reduces the concentration of glycolytic enzymes and fast-twitch muscle fibers needed for fast, powerful kicks. In other words, your ability to deliver five fast kicks in succession is a better predictor of martial art success than being able to run a marathon at an eight minute per mile pace.

Specificity

Each of your energy systems uses different muscle fibers and enzyme systems. The ability to run 10 miles means that a high percentage of slow-twitch muscle fiber, correlated enzyme structure, and energy system has been developed. However, this is not the system needed for competition success in the martial arts.

To illustrate this, consider the fact that elite endurance athletes have a vertical jump of four to six inches. In contrast, power sports feature athletes with vertical jumps five times that amount. Therefore, to be successful, training specificity must be practiced. And those elements that are not specific to the need, such as excessive endurance training, need to be reduced. If you are frustrated at the inability to achieve height in performing a jump spinning back kick, one reason could be genetic: you may not be not gifted with explosive muscle fiber (Type IIB—to be explained in the next section). However, another reason may be overtraining in endurance activities.

My purpose here is not to discourage aerobic training. It is necessary. But it needs to be in proportion to the event (your goal) or it will harm, rather than help, realization of that goal (such as competition).

Muscle Fiber Types

In terms of athletic performance, the type and size of muscle fibers determines the speed and force of an action, such as kicking and punching. To a large extent, these muscle fibers are genetically determined. Here is a summary of the basic types.

A. Type I–Endurance (slow twitch). These fibers are predominant in a long distance runner. They are fatigue resistant but have limited potential for rapid force development and low anaerobic power (won't help create fast, powerful kicks). Martial art training should not over-emphasize the recruitment or development of these fibers and enzyme systems.

B. Type II–Speed (fast twitch). While these fibers fatigue more easily, they generate much greater speed and power than aerobic type muscles, although for shorter periods of time. Type II muscles are further divided into two categories.

C. Type IIA–Intermediate. This type of fiber, because it is a derivative of Type II, creates fast and powerful movements but is not the maximum power fiber. These muscular contractions contain an oxidative component and therefore developing them involves the fast oxidative glycolytic (FOG) enzyme system. Whereas a Type I fiber person will be seen in endurance type events (distance running, swimming, etc.), a Type IIA fiber person will be seen in road cycling, or in running events such as the 880.

D. Type IIB–Anaerobic. These fibers are the least fatigue-resistant of all muscle fiber types because they are designed for short-term, maximal efforts. The enzyme system is Fast Glycolytic (FG) because there is no oxidative property to the contraction. A person with these fibers will be seen in events such as the 100 meter dash, shot-putting, or other power events.

In Chapter Five, a "field test" is provided that you can administer to yourself to approximately determine which types of fibers you possess. However, regardless of which type are predominate within you, if you want to be a (successful) martial artist you must train the energy systems and muscle fibers that support your activity. It is important to note that although muscle fibers themselves cannot be changed, the enzyme systems that guide muscular contractions can be altered. In other words, if you were born with a predominance of Type I fibers and train them with endurance types of activities, you will be successful in those activities but will see a deficiency in power type activities.

Even if you are a Type I person, you can train what Type II fibers you have, along with those enzyme systems, to maximize your Type II related performance. Of course, your individualized maximum performance may be less than that of an undertrained person who, by nature, has more Type II fibers than you. But that is no reason for you not to specifically target your desired fibers and enzymes to achieve as much as you can relative to your goals.

Energy Systems and Muscle Fiber Types Application

Let's put together what we've learned so far to further understand how success does not necessarily justify training methods. In reviewing the energy systems, you learned that your activities as a martial athlete are primarily in the phosphagen and glycolytic context (less than three minutes in duration). Even if you participate in an hour long class, this is true because most martial art classes are composed of a series of relatively high intensity movements interspersed with brief rest periods. In contrast, a continuous hour run would be an aerobic activity of moderate intensity.

By reviewing the muscle fibers, you can see that the predominant muscles used in the two martial athlete energy systems will be the Type IIA and IIB fibers. For example, a single maximum kick would use IIB fibers (no oxidation, just a maximum intensity kick). But 25 roundhouse kicks to the mid-section would use IIA fibers because some glycolytic and oxidative energy is necessary to sustain an activity of that duration and intensity.

> **If your goal is to fight three, two minute rounds in an amateur kickboxing match then an hour on the stairmaster is a complete waste**

With this in mind, let's return to the Van Damme story of an hour on the stairmaster. Due to the demands of that activity, the body will utilize the oxidative energy system with Type I muscle fibers. But is that what you want? If your goal is to fight three, two minute rounds in an amateur kickboxing match, then an hour on the stairmaster is a complete waste of time! To meet

Consider reinvesting excessive endurance training into goal specific training.

these kickboxer goals, you must train the glycolytic energy system and Type II fibers. This means you need efforts of moderately high intensity (relative to maximum heart rate) expressed in two to three minute durations, interspersed with periods of recovery.

Do you see the point here? I can't tell you how many times I've watched people spar and, after becoming winded, declare they need to "do some running" so as not to become winded. In reality, these people are doing exactly what they need to be doing; they just need more of it and to allow enough time for a training effect to occur. This is why I de-emphasize aerobic training among martial artists whose goal or system doesn't require extended duration. Bruce Lee ran minimal distances and advocated a "broken rhythm," or interval type of running which is much more transferable to the martial arts.[3] For an excellent personal example, check out how Forrest Morgan discovered the downside of running too much for the purposes of karate.[4] Forest became so endurance fit that he lost the "spring" in his kicks.

"Explosive" types of martial athletes, such as karate point fighting, frequently misinterpret the "out of breath" signal during sparring or rigorous training. Somewhere along the line, too many martial artists have been led to believe that if they're "in shape," they won't hurt; they won't run out of breath. Thus, when experiencing shortness of breath, this is misinterpreted as a need for (increased) aerobic training. In reality, any high intensity training will lead to shortness of breath (its how the phosphagen system replenishes itself). Have you ever watched a 100 meter sprinter not gasp for air at the end of a race? To be fit doesn't mean it won't hurt, it means you can do the activity. You see, it doesn't matter how well-trained you are, high intensity exercise will lead to oxygen debt. This doesn't mean do more aerobic training.

> **To be fit doesn't mean it won't hurt, it means you can do the activity.**

If you are a karate point fighter, or practice a system that makes use of similar short bursts of high intensity, and go out to run to increase your "endurance," you will actually move further away from your goal because you will be training the wrong energy and fiber systems! Nevertheless, as I've alluded to previously, someone will say, "but Don Wilson (or some other star) runs five miles a day and is a national champion." I can't argue against the national champion status. But again, by reviewing the energy and fiber systems, you can see that someone could be even more successful if development of the performance systems unrelated to the martial activity was reinvested in goal-specific training.

In Chapter Two, I will give you examples of how to create a training plan that integrates these principles to achieve your martial athlete goals. Aside from training the wrong systems (a result of not knowing the difference between energy systems and muscle fibers), another error committed by martial athletes is the assumption that certain types of training are readily transferable. For example, that swimming, running, cycling, or the stairmaster simply make one a better martial artist. They don't.

A moderate amount of aerobic activity is necessary for your general health and does, to a degree, support your martial athletics. But moderate means approximately three sessions a week of 20 minutes duration. Anything beyond that is recruiting slow-twitch enzyme systems that, by virtue of their presence in the muscle, will blunt or compromise your desire for high intensity efforts. Picture a jar with candy and fruit inside of it. If the jar is 75% full of candy, there is only 25% available for fruit. In a sense, that is what the relationship of oxidative (slow twitch) enzymes and glycolytic (fast twitch) enzyme systems is like. The presence of one, to a great extent, precludes the other.

Hit Less to Hit Harder

Let me illustrate the discrepancy between training myth and sound sport science with one of the most subtle errors committed by coaches and athletes alike. Our minds like to follow a logical process when contemplating training methods. It seems reasonable that if we want to be good competitors, we should, for example, hit the heavybag as many times and as hard as possible in each round. However, what constitutes "proper training" depends on your personal "objective."

If you want to hit as absolutely hard as possible, you should throw less punches. Sound crazy? Think for a moment about the muscle fibers and energy systems. Remember that efforts of more than six seconds in duration begin to use the glycolytic system—a partially oxidative system. The longer the

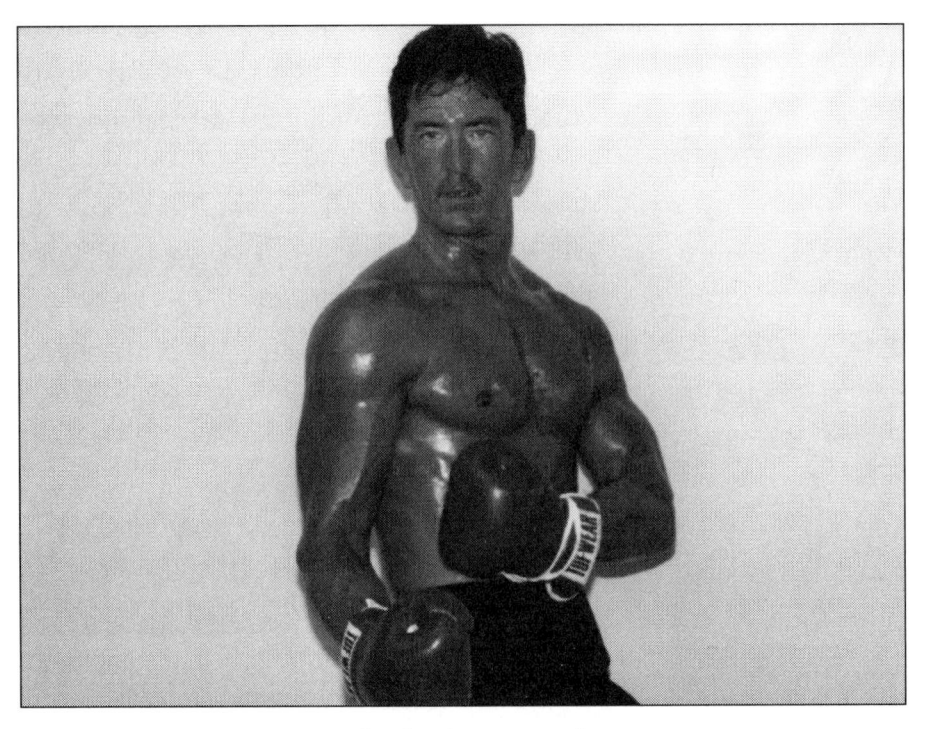

Hitting less to hit harder is part of sport science.

duration of your effort, whether hitting, sparring, or running, the more oxidative it becomes. In other words, the intensity decreases with duration. This is why a sprint is an all-out effort and distance running is performed at sub-maximal levels of intensity. The intensity is diminished in relation to the duration of the activity.

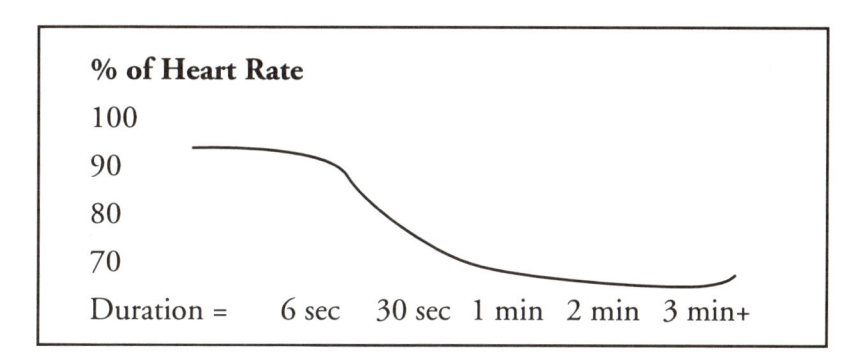

```
% of Heart Rate
100
 90
 80
 70
Duration =    6 sec   30 sec   1 min   2 min   3 min+
```

Consider the differences between weight classes in boxing. With lightweights, who typically have less Type IIB fibers (thus their smaller size), you'll see flurries of punches. While it's entertaining, it is not (comparatively) high intensity hitting. With heavyweights, who have a predominance of Type IIB fibers, you'll see less punches but they are much more lethal. Again, because the IIB fibers are not as oxidative, the heavyweights are precluded by their body type from throwing flurries like the lightweights.

How to Apply This?

To apply this knowledge, you muist first determine what it is that you are trying to achieve, i.e., what is your goal? If you're looking for that single knockout punch power, don't hit as often so that each punch you do throw will have more power. This is a function of the phosphagen system. If you want to last for 10, three minute rounds, then it is certainly appropriate to throw a large volume of punches. There's nothing wrong with that. The main point I want you to understand is that your power can be blunted or compromised by endurance types of activity. Ninety punches in two minutes is an endurance activity. The more you hit, the less Type IIB fiber enzymes you'll recruit and train.

*you can't work on speed + power at the same time.

Once you've activated the phosphagen system—which happens with even one strike—it begins to replenish itself. By decreasing the amount of strikes you throw, you allow the phosphagen system to replenish itself so that it can strike with near-maximal power again. If the duration of your strikes exceeds the phosphagen's ability to immediately replenish itself, you "trigger" the glycolytic system and, eventually, the oxidative system.

If you're like me, you may be drawn to what I call the "anaerobic haze"—that level of effort where you feel like you've had a workout (this is in the glycolytic zone, probably around 80% of your maximum heart rate). I'm not satisfied with any less. But I also realize that I'm giving away a certain amount of maximal power by pursuing these types of workouts. I want you to realize these implications as well. That is the truth of sport science, and what will distinguish you as a Total Quality Martial Artist: the intelligent pursuit of your specific objective(s).

Periodization

After you have gained an understanding of the energy systems, muscle fibers, and need for specificity in training, the next important concept in sport science and Total Quality Martial Art is periodization. High intensity training, as in the practice of martial arts, needs recovery to be effective. The intelligent way to ensure recovery is proven to be the systematic use of periodization.[5]

While many martial athletes are training the right energy system and muscle fibers, too many have nevertheless reached a plateau in their improvement. Often, these are the athletes who train either by ritual or by "feel." Those who train by ritual are athletes who create a standardized weekly and daily program of exercise and perform it week in and week out. An example of this type of athlete is someone who runs every day, lifts weights three times per week, and spars every Wednesday. That is a ritual.

In contrast, there are competitive martial artists whose training plan is decided on a daily basis, according to how they feel. If this person feels particularly good or aggressive on a certain day, the training is hard. Or, if this person doesn't feel up to it, then an easy training day is selected. Training by "feel" is a great inhibitor of athletic performance in amateur athletes. Some people are genetically gifted to the extent that they can perform successfully using this approach. But this is a very small percentage of the population.

And still others have reached a plateau because they're in a perpetual state of overtraining without adequate recovery. In order for the majority of athletes to improve, a scientifically based approach of periodization, or systematic training, is necessary. Systematic training with periodization means that an athlete performs training in accordance with an annual schedule that is comprised of alternating periods of intensity, duration, and planned recovery.[6]

These pre-planned periods of high intensity and recovery enable an athlete to avoid the pitfalls of training by ritual. One pitfall is that an athlete who trains by ritual may be very fit and conditioned but be technically underachieving because the stimulus (e.g., training load) isn't varied. A second, and more common pitfall, is overtraining, injury, or burnout because periods of recovery aren't incorporated into the training plan. Periodization, then, is a long-term emphasis on the development of your martial art future. Instead of cramming five years worth of training into one year, an incremental approach is used that realizes certain training gains take three to four years to fully develop.

Periodization can be used for all elements of a training program. With resistance training, for example, the amount of weight and number of repetitions can be varied to create ongoing improvements. In contrast, lifting the same load with the same number of repetitions three times per week means that a strength plateau will quickly be reached.

Periodization also applies to the sparring component of a training program, such as conditioning drills. Instead of always using two-minute rounds in sparring or bag work, the martial athlete should vary both the time and intensity of these rounds in order to create an ongoing training effect or improvement. To "periodize," some rounds can be performed for perhaps five minutes at a low intensity for endurance. Other rounds may be limited to thirty seconds of absolute all-out effort to train for intensity.

When the time and intensity of these components are manipulated in this fashion, there is more than conditioning occurring in the martial artist. There is progressive and varied stimulus which means that improvement will not stagnant. As long as adequate periods of recovery are integrated into the daily workouts (as well as weekly and monthly cycles), an athlete will improve and constantly move to new levels of performance and conditioning.

Some periodization models are quite complex and require a heart rate monitor to specifically gauge the level of intensity. But it can be done on a more simple basis in terms of the load, or total amount of training performed in a training cycle. For example, the simple manipulation of a ritualistic or standardized program is a means of periodization. Let's now assume that you have been using a standardized training regime of five hours per week and see how periodization works.

With your five-hour per week baseline in mind, calculate what a five percent increase [...]. Then try a 10 percent and 15 [...] weeks, respectively. Finally, calc[ulate ...] look like to serve as a recovery w[eek ...] ours this week, five hours and 20 [...] he third week—followed by a fo[urth ...] This is volume periodization. F[...] ning for recovery. Increasing th[...]

This pri[nciple ...] ing volume is used extensively i[n ...] ng, and swimming, to name a fe[w ...] of the International Sport Scienc[e ...] and Conditioning Association [...] sts serve as consultants and trainers for a variety of Olympic training programs.

[Handwritten note: WEEK #1 - 5 HRS. / WEEK #2 - 5½ HRS. / WEEK #3 - 6 HRS. / WEEK #4 - 4 HRS.]

Periodization and Underachieving

The emphasis here is that without periodization you will not reach your potential, but will be under-achieving. To further understand this principle of under-achieving, let's consider the implications of the General Adaptation Syndrome (GAS). When someone begins a training program, the human body initially reacts in shock. A new demand has been placed on it. After the shock stage, the body then begins the process of adapting to the new stress.

This process of adaptation varies among athletes but it can take from three weeks to several months. If the training program remains constant in terms of time, intensity, and frequency (a ritual), the body will eventually fully adapt to the demands of the program. This is called an adaptation. Once this has occurred, an athlete reaches a third stage which is characterized as boredom. This is a plateau wherein the training demands that were so shocking to the body in the beginning are no longer capable of stimulating a training effect (e.g., improvement) because the body has adapted to the ritualized training demands. A person could be running 10 miles a day and still be "bored," in terms of improvement.

This is where the principle of technical under-achieving arises. Although a very spartan program of running, weight training, and sparring may be performed faithfully each day, if you do not alter the amount of time, intensity, or frequency of those workouts, the program will no longer cause improvements. There may be improvements in technique, but in terms of conditioning improvement stagnates.

Sport science addresses this GAS phenomenon through the concept of periodization. According to this approach, you will vary either the volume (total time), intensity, or frequency of the training program so that the body is alternately stimulated by increasing demands followed by subsequent periods of recovery.

Training Cycles

In systematic training, these planned periods are referred to as training cycles with one or two peaks during the year. Since the human body is only capable of perhaps two peaks annually,[7] it is important to plan our cycles so that we are in top condition for our desired event. Broadly speaking, there are three training cycles.

The first is called the "macrocycle" and refers to the overall, annual training plan. The second is termed the "mesocycle" and refers to a period covering several weeks to several months of training. And finally there is the "microcycle" that describes the training that will take place within a given week. By planning training and using these broad cycles, periodization goes on throughout the year so that the body is either receiving new demands or recovering.

To put it simply, periodization means that the volume and intensity of any program, regardless of the relative success against competitors, must be manipulated to create continuous, individual improvement. In application, ritualistic training is technically under-achieving since an improvement plateau is unintentionally created. We'll examine these training cycles more closely in Chapter Two.

Chapter Review

In this chapter we have initiated the important step of gathering sport science data in our model of Total Quality Martial Arts. This data includes the important distinction between the three energy systems, different types of muscle fibers, and need for training specificity if we're to realize our goals as a martial athlete. We've also learned that even with the right training methods, there is a need for periodization to promote improvements and ensure that we properly recover from training. This periodization means that our training program should be divided into cycles of high and low intensity and feature changes in the volume or total time demands of training.

These sport science facts demonstrate that success does not justify training methods. Some athletes are successful despite themselves and misunderstood training theory. Don't accept mediocre returns on your training investment. Train right and overachieve your potential.

CHAPTER TWO

CREATING THE ANNUAL TRAINING PLAN

"The surest way to make a mission impossible is to make it invisible."
—ANONYMOUS

To be a Total Quality martial artist is an invitation to base your training program on established sport science and Total Quality Management principles. This means that you train the right energy and muscle systems (sport science) and develop the skill of recording and measuring your performance (TQM). In order to adopt this scientific and process-oriented approach, you must become intentional in your training. In other words, to reach your absolute maximum potential, you can't just train hard all the time or train according to how you feel. There's a place for "feel" in training, but it should not be the primary component of your decision making.

Training by "feel" is detrimental for two reasons. First, it is generally a great inhibitor of realizing genetic potential. It is extremely unlikely that you would ever try to systematically lift 105% of your one repetition maximum (1RM), perform intervals, or basically do anything of enduring athletic value because you "feel" like it. The tendency is do what we we're comfortable with, not reach beyond that.

Secondly, "feel" is an inadequate indicator of pending injury. One of the great lessons I learned in cycling is that a successful athlete must anticipate his or her needs, not wait until they are felt. For instance, if you wait until you feel thirsty, you're probably already experiencing some level of dehydration. If I haven't been sparring at the *dojo* for a while, I don't wait until I feel blisters on my feet to stop training for the night. I did one time and couldn't walk right for a week! If my feet aren't calloused, I know I better start tapering off after about 45 minutes or I'm in for trouble.

Intentional and Systematic

To be intentional means to become deliberate and that means you need a training plan. An annual, systematic plan offers you many advantages distinct from the "go hard," "train by feel," or "follow the pack" programs. Before we examine how to create a plan, let's review the benefits.

1. A reduction of both over- and under-training.
Numerous martial athletes work at such high levels of consistent intensity that they become ill, injured, or stagnant in their progress. Consistent over-training can, and often does, lead to a perpetual state of non-recovery. In fact, anaerobic sports (such as martial arts) have the highest percentage of overtraining (77%).[1] On the other hand, some athletes are not achieving a high level of benefit because they are not exercising hard enough. An annual plan with programmed intensity levels will help you escape these errors.

2. More fat-burning exercise.
To paraphrase an old maxim, "all fat is not burned equally." Certain (high) levels of intensity rely exclusively on carbohydrates as an energy source while lower levels rely on a mixture of carbohydrate and fat or exclusively fat. Have you ever seen a dedicated "aerobicizer" who becomes very (aerobically) fit after months of classes but still carries visible body fat? This may be due to an exercise intensity that burns more carbohydrate than fat. By following a systematic program, you can target specific fat-burning types of exercise and (appropriate) intensity levels.

3. The ability to perform really hard work.
As you learn to integrate the essential training components of Total Quality

Establishing, then reviewing, an annual plan with younger martial athletes it the Total Quality Way.

Martial Arts, you will be able to go harder and faster than ever before. Many athletes, without coaching or a plan, tend to exercise just below or right at the lactate threshold (this term will be explained under "Training Components"). Generally speaking, this accounts for both overtraining and undertraining. It is overtraining in the sense that athletes stuck in this intensity zone aren't incorporating recovery time. It is undertraining in the sense that intelligently trained athletes should be able to perform supra-maximal efforts, such as 105% of a target maximum heart rate.

4. A personalized plan!

As explained in Chapter One, too many athletes attempt to replicate the formulas of elite superstars, reasoning that if it works for the elite then it certainly will work for them. If you haven't discovered it already, you will unfortunately find that elite athletes' programs often contradict one another and, frequently, will overwhelm an amateur athlete's ability with disproportionate training demands. A personalized, annual systematic training plan is based on science, not anecdote, and will enable you to maximize your own unique potential.

Now that we've reviewed some of the benefits of a training plan, let's review the steps that will lead to your personalized version.

Volume of Training

The first step in designing your training plan is to determine your amount of previous annual training. We can't even begin to talk about what you will do until we determine what you have done. The reasoning for this is simple. I can list all sorts of training options for you but if the options add up to say, 10 hours per week, and you're accustomed to five hours per week, we're inviting overtraining, injury, or illness. This is extremely important and yet another reason why you can't just jump into the most recent training program you've read about in your favorite magazine. Sure, some superstars may work-out three hours per day, but that isn't how it started—that's the achieved level.

If you're one of the fortunate few who have maintained a semblance of a training log, you should be able to approximate how many annual hours you spent training last year. If a log was not maintained (most likely) but a fairly standard weekly training schedule was performed, that weekly training plan can be extrapolated to estimate the total amount of annual hours. For example, if a routine of six hours of exercise per week was performed, multiply this amount by the total amount of exercise weeks in the previous year remembering to subtract vacations, illness, or other breaks. A standard six hour exercise week multiplied by 50 weeks would be 300 annual hours. It should be noted that the "standard" exercise week includes the total amount of all exercise, not just martial arts. The majority of amateur athletes will be in the range of 100 to 300 hours annually.

Once you've developed your estimate, this figure will become the basis for the first year of systematic training. Subsequent years can feature a 10% to 15% increase in the amount of annual training hours. But in the beginning, don't over stress the body by making a huge change in your annual training volume.

Training Cycles

Even if you are training the right systems and fibers discussed in Chapter One, you can burnout, become injured, or plateau in your improvements if the training volume isn't periodized into training cycles. In addition, it is only possible to physically peak once or twice a year. So, an effective training plan will enable you to practice safely, realize improvements, and bring you into peak form for your desired goals.

In systematic training, the annual training plan (with total amount of hours) is viewed as the "macrocycle." Dividing the year into several broad components become the "mesocycles." The actual training week, then, is referred to as the "microcycle." After establishing the (annual) macrocycle of training volume, your next step is to plan the mesocycles. Let's look at the broad mesocycles of a point-tournament fighter whose emphasis is on the spring and fall tournaments.

MESOCYCLE	EXAMPLE DATES
Recovery	June 1–July 31
Build I	Aug. 1–31
Intensity I	Sep. 1–Dec. 20
Recovery	Dec. 21–31
Build II	Jan. 1–31
Intensity II	Feb. 1–May 30

Each of these periods establishes the general direction that training will take in terms of intensity, duration, and frequency. One of the primary keys to these mesocycles is the intensity of training.

As an example, consider sparring. In the recovery stage that follows a spring of tournaments, you probably won't spar at all. This is a period of psychological and physical rest. Then, in the "Build I" stage, you would begin to perform perhaps three, three minute rounds of medium intensity (breathing is still controlled). This begins preparing you for more intense sparring and competition later in the cycle. Next, in the intensity stage, you begin performing all-out efforts for use in competition. And, during the Christmas season, another recovery stage is employed where sparring should be "light," or significantly below normal thresholds. This way you continue to refine skills but you provide your mind, heart, and muscles with some needed rest. In turn, you become even more hungry to go hard again during the "Build II" and "Intensity II" stages of the late winter and spring.

This principle of varying the intensity is used with each component of your training, including technique, lactate, resistance, and aerobic conditioning (to be explained shortly). The important point to realize is that, once again, you can't just create the "ideal" training week and perform it year round. Mesocycles provide you with the structure to vary training intensity, duration, and frequency throughout the year to ensure effective and safe training.

Calculating Mesocycles

To calculate your mesocycle, divide your annual training volume into distinct periods of varying time, intensity, and duration (although this is not an easy task). When I first began practicing and coaching systematic training, I manually calculated these cycles. This can be tedious because of all the different percentages assigned to the various mesocycles. For instance, a basic 300 hour annual plan with detailed mesocycles can be divided into the percentages of relative training time shown in the table on page 31.

As you can see, each mesocycle has a percentage of the total annual hours. The varying percentage of the annual work hours is due, again, to periodization. Instead of simply performing the same volume of exercise week in and week out, in systematic training you vary the volume so that the body is overloaded and then allowed recovery.

In the next step, these mesocycles are further broken down by percentages to determine how much exercise should be performed in a given week. For example, since a total of six percent of the annual hours are in Cycle One of the Build I stage, a total of 18 exercise hours are performed during the first four week cycle (18 = 6% of 300). Following the determination that 18 hours will be performed in a four week stage, workload percentages are used to determine how many hours are performed each week. In the example of the Build I stage, four different percentages are sequentially used for each week. As an example,

PHYSICAL CONSIDERATIONS

MESOCYCLE	STAGE	%YEAR HOURS	ACTUAL HOURS
1	Build I	6	18
2	Build II	7	21
3	Build III	8	24
4	Build IV	7	21
5	Build V	9	27
6	Intensity I	9	27
7	Intensity II	10	30
8	Intensity III	11	33
9	Intensity IV	9	27
10	Peak	8	24
11	Competition I	7	21
12	Competition II	6	18
13	Recovery	3	9
TOTAL		100%	300

the percentages 23%, 26%, 29%, and 22% will be used. Those 18 hours are thus broken down in the following manner:

Mesocycle 1 (Build I) **Total Hours = 18**
Week 1   4 hrs, 14 min. (23%)
Week 2   5 hrs, 8 min. (26%)
Week 3   5 hrs, 22 min. (29%)
Week 4   3 hrs, 56 min. (22%)

As you can see, these calculations can become quite intricate even to develop one plan if done manually. Think of how much work it would take to develop plans for several martial athletes! Fortunately, you have a choice in how your mesocycles may be calculated.

Three Options

You can create a personalized annual training plan with detailed mesocycles by one of three means. The first is to create it manually. In order to fully understand the principles and relationship between planning factors, this might be desirable for a year or two of planning. But there are more time-efficient options.

Another option is to use preplanned worksheets such as those offered by Fred Koch in his book *Strength Training for Sports*.[2] These preplanned worksheets include plans for karate as well as running and weightlifting and numerous other activities. Another option, if you're comfortable with computer technology, is to use software such as "Training Design," Version 6.1 by Gary Winckler (see Appendix for ordering information). This tool enables you to plan training programs, prescribe workouts, then record and analyze them for future planning—an excellent example of the Total Quality approach.

If it hasn't occurred to you yet, perhaps the biggest obstacle to adopting and using a personalized annual training plan will be the *dojo* itself. That's right. The very source of your martial art activity may do more to undermine your systematic, sport science based efforts than any other factor! The reason for this is quite simple: the *dojo* is designed to accommodate large groups of people at a single occasion. Furthermore, the training sessions are determined by the instructor. This is why Bruce Lee stated we should have our own training schedule besides our activities at the *dojo*.[3]

If you are practicing a systematic schedule that calls for perhaps a five hour recovery week and you go to the *dojo* on a night when you already have five hours of exercise completed that week, you risk overtraining by participating—especially if it's an intensity session. Instead of just following the pack, you must creatively decide how to maintain the integrity of your plan without disrupting the *dojo*. For instance, you can volunteer to referee sparring matches or assist with instruction on these occasions. The important thing to realize is that you cannot blindly follow the *dojo* training schedule and be a Total Quality martial artist. To follow the guidelines of your individual training plan means communicating with your instructor to let him or her know where you are in your training and discussing alternatives if the *dojo* training session doesn't match your program at that point.

Training Components

After the determination of annual training volume and selection of mesocycles, the next crucial step is to determine what specific types of training should be used to develop as a martial athlete. As we learned in Chapter One, the anaerobic energy systems (phosphagen and glycolytic) and fast-twitch muscle fibers are primary targets for development. Regardless of your system, there are six important areas that are included in the training plan. These six areas include skills, resistance training, lactate conditioning, aerobic conditioning, absorption, and flexibility.

Skills are the fundamental techniques of the art you practice. For karate, this means kicks, punches, and blocks. If your aim is street self-defense, it may mean joint-locks and grappling. At a minimum, three sessions of 30 minutes each should be performed each week to develop these skills, regardless of your training stage. This guideline provides enough specific training to adequately reinforce the desired skill and yet provides time for the other essential components of an integrated plan.

Skill training is a top priority as a martial artist, but not the only training needed.

Resistance training makes good martial artists better, as black belt Duane Anstaett demonstrates.

Resistance training, also known as weightlifting, should be incorporated into your plan in order to strengthen the joints and muscles used in the martial arts. It is my own opinion that strength training is often the "missing component" needed to create a total training plan for most martial artists. Forget this stuff about "it makes big, inflexible muscles." Resistance training can be performed to build faster, stronger, or endurance-trained muscles. It depends on the type of training. Does Van Damme look inflexible to you?

Because strength training is so important, Chapter Three outlines the essential components of a plan that will not only make you more successful, but also less prone to injury. For the moment, however, let's address the following considerations.

In general, the amount of repetitions in the training set will determine the type of training effect (when considered with the amount of weight). If you lift with more than 12 repetitions in a set, you are primarily training local muscular endurance. You won't get big but will have very toned, fatigue-resistance muscles. If you lift with repetition sets of eight to 12, you get a mix of endurance and strength training. This is the range where many bodybuilders exercise. And if you lift heavy weights with three to six repetitions, you are training for strength.

Toning and strengthening the muscles is of paramount importance and can make the difference between winning or losing, resilience or injury. For example, squats and lunges are extremely effective for the lower body and are beneficial to any system of martial art. Or, to develop rapid force movement in the upper body, you can practice lat pull-downs, biceps curls, and bent-over rows. These are fundamental exercises used by wrestlers to develop critical upper body skills.

If you absolutely are unable to enjoy "iron" based resistance training, you must, as a minimum, perform some isometric exercises such as push-ups, pull-ups, and various abdominal exercises. This will at least promote muscle tone and some strength, though not as much as iron resistance training.

Lactate conditioning means training yourself to handle periods of high intensity.[4] This is part of the glycolytic energy system discussed in Chapter One. When we exercise at a fairly high level of intensity, lactate is what slows down our muscle contractions and causes us to breath heavy. In sport science, the term lactate threshold is used to describe the point where the production of lactate from muscular contractions causes decreases in our performance (the reduced contractions and heavy breathing).

But the lactate threshold can be raised by training, which is why your training plan should include periods of planned high intensity. For example, begin exercising and then increase the intensity level to the point you begin to slightly gasp (or pant) for air. Then sustain that intensity level for two to three minute sets with 40 seconds to one minute recovery periods. This is lactate conditioning. The recovery periods are important so that your body learns to absorb and reuse lactate. Five, three-minute rounds performed three times a week develops this capability sufficient for local competition or the demands of most *dojos*.

Aerobic conditioning, on the other hand, means you are at a (reduced) intensity level greater than three minutes, generally the type where you can sustain the exercise up to 20 minutes in duration. These are two different types of conditioning (lactate and aerobic) and should not be confused. One way to determine which type of conditioning you are performing is to make a very general, subjective assessment about the level of intensity. If you can comfortably talk during exercise, you're at the aerobic level. On the other hand, if breathing is labored, you're at the glycolytic level.

Another, and more precise, method is to make an (intensity) determination based on your heart rate and then train in certain "zones," generally describing which energy system you are training in relative to your heart rate. You can use the following general formula to determine those zones.

Step 1: Subtract age from 220. This is Maximum Heart Rate

Step 2: Take the answer from step one and calculate.

Zone 1, recovery   MHR. x .60 = _115_ to MHR. x .70 = _134_

Zone 2, aerobic   MHR. x .71 = _136_ to MHR. x .75 = _144_

Zone 3, intensity   MHR. x .76 = _146_ to MHR. x .81 = _156_

Zone 4, glycolytic   MHR. x .82 = _157_ to MHR. x .90 = _173_

Zone 5, lactate threshold   MHR. x .91 = _175_ to MHR. _192_

Depending on how technological you want to be, you can either use a heart rate monitor to assess you're precise number or you can put a finger on either your wrist or carotid artery in the neck for six seconds and add a zero—that's your current heart rate.

Despite my caution about too much aerobic conditioning for the martial athlete, it is a vital component of your training plan—when proportionate to your goal. Aerobic conditioning is necessary for your general health. I recently opened the pages of a popular martial arts magazine and noted that four renowned masters all died before age 60 of various heart problems. Perform aerobic conditioning: three sessions of 20 minute duration per week is sufficient.

What we have covered thus far are the "active" elements of your training plan. Most athletes get excited about this part of training. But it is also important to note at this point that all gains from training—whether from resis-

Partner assisted stretching achieves maximum flexibility.

tance, lactate, or aerobic conditioning—are made in the recovery portion of your life. That is, the time between training sessions. In other words, if you work out hard for two hours today, the effect is realized after your muscles and energy systems have had an opportunity to incorporate that stimulus into gains. Unfortunately, too many athletes overlook this necessity and, after seeing gains in some area, reason that "if a little is good, a whole lot more is better." This can lead to injury, burnout, or overtraining. (I offer some important thoughts about the need for absorption (rest) at the end of this chapter.)

Your essential training components must, therefore, also include "passive" components to facilitate recovery and make training gains. This is the deliberate plan to allow your body periods of recovery between workouts and on a daily basis (absorption). This is the part that is deliberately designed to be easy. Techniques such as stationary cycling, steam baths, massage, and stretching will help you absorb your training.

Flexibility is the fundamental practice of systematically increasing suppleness and joint range of motion. Technically speaking, suppleness refers to the muscles (elasticity) and flexibility refers to the joints (mobility), although "flexibility" is generally used to refer to the muscles. Furthermore, it is important to note that both suppleness and flexibility are best achieved following the workout—not before. Our training culture frequently says "let's practice flexibility before sparring" and after the session we stop cold and get ready to go home. This is improper training.

Instead, what occurs prior to the exercise session is simply warm-up wherein you raise body temperature, improve circulation, and prepare for physical activity. After the body is warm is the time when true deep stretching should occur. This means 10 to 15 minutes of planned "flexibility" exercises after the training session. I incorporate this into resistance training sessions between sets to maximize time management.

Component Skills

Moving from the annual plan to the mesocycles to the training components now leads us to the specific activities that you will practice on a weekly basis.

Training components may include nunchakus, weights, and boxing gloves.

PHYSICAL CONSIDERATIONS

With the exception of "lactate conditioning and/or skills," these alternatives are universal to all martial athletes. Every athlete needs some resistance and aerobic training, along with absorption. The lactate and skills, however, will be designed according to the system you practice. The following outline is for a karate fighter.

LACTATE CONDITIONING and/or SKILLS:	RESISTANCE TRAINING:
Technique training	Weights
Sparring and Focus Mitts	Technique training under water
Jump rope	Hand instruments (grips, etc.)
Heavybag	Push-ups, pull-ups, sit-ups
Plyometrics	
AEROBIC:	**ABSORPTION:**
Run	Stationary cycling
Cycle	Walking
Swim	Massage
Stairmaster	Stretching

If you are not a karate fighter but a sport judo player, then you will insert things like "throws" instead of "focus mitts." Likewise, "tumbling" might be used instead of the "heavybag," if you don't practice a striking art but perform a throwing art like aikido. You know your system. Pick the essential core elements of that system, list them, and then systematically train them every week. The point in listing the component skills is to ensure that you target all the areas necessary for health and success on a weekly basis. An example of how these might fit together is provided in the "sample schedule" on page 40.

Sample Schedule

Annual Hours = 300
Cycle = Build I
Week = 5 hours, 30 minutes

Mon	Tues	Wed	Thu	Fri	Sat	Sun
Aerobic .20 (a.m.)	Res/Flex .30 (a.m.)	Aerobic .20 (noon)	Res/Flex .30 (a.m.)		Aerobic .20 (noon)	Absorption (off)
Technique 1.0 (p.m.- class)		Lactate .40 (p.m. - bag)	Technique 1.0 (p.m.- class)	Lactate .40 Technique .10 (p.m.)	Res/Flex .30 (p.m.)	
Totals: 1.20	.30	1.0	1.0	.50	.50	= 5.30

Training Mix Analysis

1. Technique: 1.40 total; moderate intensity, exact precision

2. Lactate: 1.20 total; 3 minute rounds with 1 minute intervals

3. Aerobic: 1.0 total; medium pace with 3 to 4 "bursts" (40 yards)

4. Resistance: 1.30 total; 3 sets of 10 reps at 80 of 1 rep max; 6 exercises

5. Flexibility: incorporated into resistance training sessions

6. Absorption: Two 24 breaks, one day off

Lifeplanning

As you create your personalized training plan, it is important to look at the entire picture of your life. While we may read of martial athletes who train three hours a day, their program is not necessarily best for you. A particular athlete may have three hours available to train on a daily basis because that's what he or she does for a living. Assuming that you are an amateur (or even a martial art instructor), three hours is perhaps out of the question. In turn, we need "lifeplanning"—a big picture look at the demands of our lives and what amount of time is truly available for martial art training.

In other words, if your job, school, or family commitments leave you with perhaps five hours a week to train, it would be silly to plan an eight hour workout week. You will only end up frustrated. Instead, you really need to take a precise look at how much time you have available—and be precise. It needs to be assessed as accurately as balancing your checkbook. Don't accept generalized conclusions like "sure, I've got two hours a day to train." Really sit down and calculate the amount of time available.

> **Training has to be proportionate to your life and that includes work, family, and similar commitments so that "overloading" is avoided.**

Contrary to some of the myths surrounding sports and training, it is not absolutely necessary to exercise daily to achieve or maintain fitness. You can be fit, and even compete at the amateur level, on approximately three to four sessions per week. If you can train more and want to maximize your potential, that's great! But to be a Total Quality martial artist, training has to be proportionate to your life, and that includes work, family, and similar commitments so that "overloading" is avoided. With that premise, try determining how much training time you have available on a weekly basis. To be as precise as balancing your checkbook, you should start with the overall hours available in a week (168) and then subtract the time associated with your core life activities. For example, subtract the time needed for sleep, work, commuting, meals, household, responsibilities, friends, leisure, and whatever else represents your "normal" week.

Let's assume you determine that you have approximately four hours available to train each week, even though you really need about eight hours to meet the goal of success in regional competition. Should you abandon your martial athlete goals? Should you quit your job? Should you ignore your family? To be successful at life planning means that to compensate the difference between the time available and the perceived amount needed to compete, our lifeplanning must include creative use of your time. I call this "training in the margins."

Training in the Margins

During a typical work week, I estimate that on paper I have probably four hours available for training (Monday through Friday). But I routinely train for up to eight hours during those five days. How? By using the margins. If we look at our martial training in a "box" then we'll assume that any training means very distinct activities such as driving to the dojo, changing clothes, working out, driving home, etc. (about a two hour ordeal for a one hour workout). But if we view training as a free flow experience, there are numerous opportunities to train in the margins. Let me explain.

If I take my daughter to piano lessons (which last a half hour) I don't just sit in the car and wait. I get out and stretch. Or I may run, do push-ups, or any number of things depending on what I'm doing after we leave the piano lessons (I won't do something sweaty if the next activity would make that inappropriate). That's what I call training in the "margins." If you look at your life, you'll find there are numerous opportunities for "margins" training.

For example, let's say that once you've outlined your training plan, you determine a goal of 30 minutes stretching per day (good luck!). There are many opportunities to do this during the day. How about five minutes during a break at work or between classes? How about 10 minutes when you find yourself waiting for a late appointment? Or another 15 minutes while you watch the opening of Monday Night Football? There are a wide range of possibilities if you don't "box" or compartmentalize your view of training. Some people would look at the six training components outlined in this chapter and think that they must all be performed in the same training session, one after the other. Actually, each component can be addressed individually which enhances your "lifeplanning."

Split your training up into manageable pieces and maximize the margins. I average one-and-a-half to two hours of training per day, but almost never at one time. Given my commitments to family, work, and life I couldn't say "I'll train from 7:00 to 9:00 PM each night." That would interfere with my other commitments. Instead, I may run for 20 minutes and do push-ups and sit-ups at lunch. After dinner with the family, I may do 30 minutes of lactate conditioning on the heavy bag. Later in the evening, while talking with my spouse or watching the news, I'll do stretching and flexibility exercises. When the day is done, I've recorded an hour and a half of training but only 30 minutes of the day were actually "boxed." In other words, that 30 minutes on the heavybag were the only segregated or "boxed" training minutes. I folded running, isometrics, and stretching into the margins of other activities.

These examples demonstrate how it is possible to train for your goals without the rest of your life going to pot. Don't sweat it out for three hours a night at the *dojo* if that means neglecting your work, school, or family. Lifeplanning means meeting the commitments of your whole life in a balanced way; not neglecting things to (exclusively) focus on training. Yet it also means not using life commitments as an excuse for insufficient training. The key to the balance between these two extremes may well rest in your ability to train in the margins.

I don't know what "margins" are available to you, but here are some examples of "margins" training I have successfully used. While driving: hand strength, deep breathing, and listening to physiology tapes. While standing in lines: toe raises, visualization, muscle flexing, and deep breathing. And perhaps most importantly, using the "margins" time while supporting other people's activities (such as waiting on children at soccer practice) for brief periods of running, stretching, kicking, and the like. There are many opportunities to train in the margins.

The real art in developing a systematic, periodized training schedule is to integrate the various aspects we've reviewed (energy systems and muscle fibers in Chapter One; annual hours, mesocycles, training components, training skills, lifeplanning, and the margins from this chapter) into a comprehensive plan. Clearly, some of this can be planned by using a preplanned or computerized training schedule such as those I've previously discussed. But due to the lifeplanning and margin aspects, you will still have to develop some of the training schedule yourself. The "Sample Schedule" is an example of how a particular week might look for the Total Quality martial artist. Please keep in mind that this is only one week and doesn't tell the whole story of a periodized schedule.

For Those Who Don't Compete

I realize that many readers may have no desire for tournaments or competition. In fact, in some martial arts, competition is actually discouraged because it's viewed as contrary to certain spiritual goals. Philosophical arguments aside, even if you don't compete (for whatever reason), you need a systematic annual training plan. If you don't, you are vulnerable to injuries, burnout, or lack of progress. Remember, any training ritual, whether for competition or not, falls short of sport science if it does not incorporate periodization, recovery, and other sport science principles. So yes, even if your practice is tai chi, you need periods of overload (in training volume) and periods of recovery. You also need lifeplanning and training in the margins. The volume and intensity of training might not be as much as the competitive martial athlete, but the principles are the same. Total Quality Martial Arts is for every martial athlete, competitive or not.

The Waning Art of Absorption

Have you pictured yourself as a member of the U.S. Olympic Team? To get there, you would have to practice the art of absorption I alluded to earlier. Have you wondered what it would be like to reach all of your potential whether it landed you in the Olympics or not? Again, you would have to practice the art of absorption. It is the newest word in sport science for emphasizing recovery from exercise so that you grow in strength, power, and speed.

Since it's sometimes easier to learn what something is by defining what it is not, let's review the opposite of absorption: overtraining. Overtraining is a physical or mental state wherein exercise becomes detrimental, tearing you down instead of building you up. Successful martial athletes avoid this, even with flexibility training. Bill Wallace, the great champion, says he stretches daily, but only hard twice a week. Christine Bannon-Rodriguez performs light stretching daily with only one heavy day of stretching per week. In essence, they are "absorbing," i.e., allowing the body to recover.

In contrast, those who go heavy every day eventually display the signs of overtraining. You should thoughtfully review the following list to see if you display any of these signs: recurrent injuries, repeated illnesses, consistent soreness or fatigue, decrease in body weight, loss of appetite, difficulty sleeping, or a general loss of motivation to exercise.

If you have one or more of these signs, you may be like many other ambitious athletes, including past Olympic hopefuls, who consistently perform rigorous exercise. Intense exercise is not a problem in and of itself. The human body was designed for it. In fact, if you manage training and stress correctly they will lead you to the ultimate in health and fitness. Used incorrectly, however, they bring disaster.

That is why I am concluding this chapter on creating an annual training plan with an admonition to make sure that you plan recovery time. In fact, based on years of carefully recording various training plans and their effects on human performance, an advisory board of the Olympic committee has determined a startling fact: the performance of top athletes is more often thwarted by overtraining than undertraining. Therefore, absorption needs to be a critical component of your training plan.

Absorption Manages Lactic Acid

As discussed in Chapter One and earlier in this chapter, lactic acid is a byproduct of high intensity training such as that performed in the martial arts. It occurs in any sport where heart rate is elevated to near maximal levels. If you have never heard of this exercise-induced chemical before you have no doubt experienced it. Along with hydroxproline, it is what makes you sore the morning after a hard workout.

As an analogy, picture flowing water that freezes in certain temperatures. Lactic acid "flows" during exercise and is partially used to continue high-intensity training. If training stops abruptly and an effort is not made to purge it, in a sense lactic acid "freezes" in your muscles and joints. Among other reasons, this may contribute to a state of overtraining expressed in the symptoms previously discussed (recurrent injuries, consistent soreness, fatigue, and so on).

What sport scientists have concluded is probably what you have seen in yourself and your peers. Competitive athletes have special goals in mind. It could be winning a tournament or achieving a black belt. And with a goal, the tendency is to train as much as possible. But too much training can make your goal elusive.

By practicing the art of absorption, you are deliberately allowing your body to recover. The human body is a sensitive and complex system that can be trained to the point where training has no effect. That happens when the body can no longer absorb the stimulus. It is like the boy who cried wolf so often people began to ignore him. With excessive stimulation, the body may begin to ignore the demands imposed by you and begin a series of "red flags" like injuries, illness, and fatigue. So, the art we are talking about here is, in one sense, a straightforward prescription of "train + rest = improved performance."

No One Formula

There is no one formula that all athletes can adopt to ensure recovery and the art of absorption within the annual training plan. With Olympic hopefuls, coaches use a wide range of tools to determine each individual's state of recovery and physical health. Some of these tools include sophisticated equipment not available to the average amateur athlete. Some are inexpensive, such as measuring the waking pulse rate.

Whether you have a coach or are self-coached, the difficulty is that individual athletes recover at different rates. With some, a programmed day off each week provides enough recovery. With others, two days may be necessary. These individual recovery rates are the result of numerous variables. If you work at a desk or attend school during the day, that may serve as enough recovery from your vigorous nightly workouts. If you perform physical labor during the day in addition to high intensity martial art training, you may need two days off per week to compensate the demands on your body.

Some Alternatives

Although there is not a formula or standard method for the amount of time necessary to recover, members of various Olympic teams practice some methods that can also help you. Here are some ideas.

1. Stationary cycling. Numerous athletes pedal easily on an indoor trainer for 15 minutes in the morning and evening to rid the body of lactic acid and other toxins. This is done at 50% to 60% of the target heart rate normally used for rigorous training (which means it's not aerobic).

2. Massage. Not many of us have a personal masseur available. But even a visit once a week to your local favorite can be helpful. Many athletes practice self-massage. To do this, lie on your back with your legs resting against a wall and gently rub them down.

3. Stretching. Remember: you should warm-up prior to a session and stretch afterward. Deep stretching of cold muscles can cause minor tears.

4. Hot-tub or steam rooms. The heat generated by these two activities helps the body "flush" itself of lactic acid and other toxins in your body. It is also the most fun of these four alternatives!

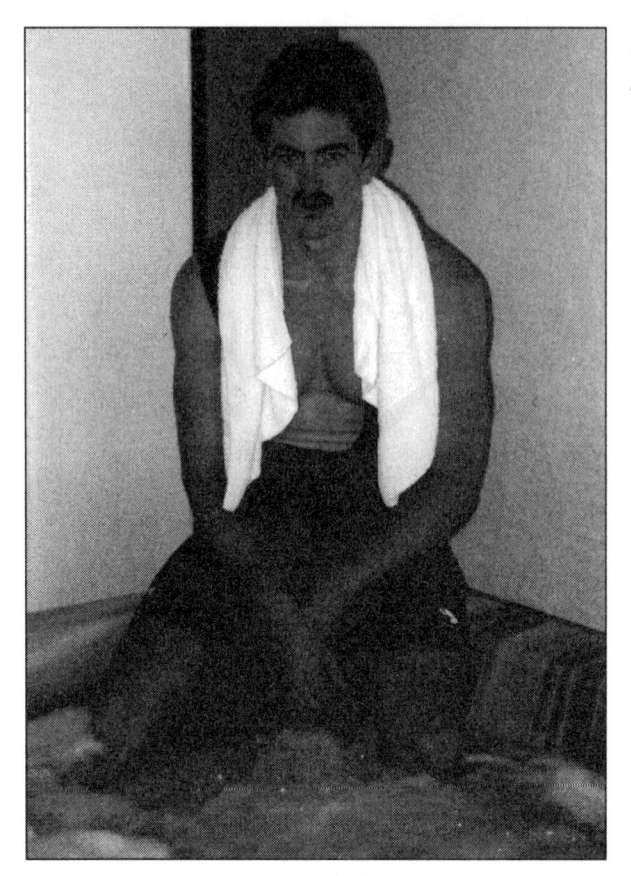

Hot tubs are a welcome relief after grueling training.

A lot of sport literature addresses the need for recovery. Most of us like to read the parts about developing bigger muscles or faster kicks and skip the portions that describe the need to recover from these training demands. You may be surviving on little to no recovery right now. But eventually it will take its toll. Instead, you can increase your performance and safeguard yourself against overtraining and injuries if you practice absorption. It is required of the Olympians. It will work for you. Absorption is what makes your training plan complete.

CHAPTER THREE

STRENGTH AND NUTRITION MATTERS

"You have to have that strength."
—Jeff Speakman

The art or system doesn't matter. From tai chi to shotokan, from aikido to taekwondo, your martial art performance can be maximized through strength training. There are a lot of myths about this topic. Some are about fears that it can make you too tight. Not according to Jean Claude VanDamme or Jeff Speakman.[1] They both practice it, have the physiques to show it, and physically express their arts in a fluid, graceful manner.

Other myths exist about how much to lift; confusing the amount of repetitions necessary to target strength, endurance, or mass like a bodybuilder. In this chapter I'll present the essential aspects of this topic to help you maximize your art. I consider strength training the "missing component" because it is my perception that most martial artists get plenty of technique and flexibility training through attendance at classes. Likewise, most committed athletes perform some type of aerobic training as well. But strength training is often neglected either because of an unawareness of the benefits, misconceptions, or simply being designated as a low priority. In contrast, research demonstrates that resistance training will not only make you stronger, but improve the speed of punching as well.[2] It has also been demonstrated that the trunk and lower extremities account for 76% of the effort in delivering a straight jab.[3] As a result, you need resistance training of both the upper and lower body.

Benefits

Let's start with some sound reasons you need to begin strength training as soon as possible. Please note that this isn't some type of recommendation for "cross training." Strength training needs to be a fundamental component if you want maximize performance—not a "cross over" afterthought. The best benefit is that it will improve your art.

In the striking arts, many times roundhouse kicks aren't delivered as hard or as long as desired due to a weakness in the hamstrings, not the quadriceps (as many people assume). This is because antagonist muscles (hamstrings in this case) will contract or stop prematurely to prevent hyperextension in your kicks. In other words, your quadriceps (the agonists) may be strong, but a muscle imbalance between the two groups used to deliver the roundhouse will

Strengthening the hamstrings with leg curls enhances powerful kicks.

compromise your performance. Similar reasons exist for those of the non-striking arts. If you practice judo, you may be able to throw your opponent, but having the strength necessary for certain holds can be another matter.

Strength training will also reduce the incidence of injuries, and, when they occur, their extent. Using myself as an example, due to very well-developed muscles in my legs, at one time I experienced a mild tear of my medial ligament instead of it being shred by the incident that caused the injury. My doctor said my muscle strength saved me months of recovery that would have been necessary with less muscular protection.

Finally, bigger muscles burn more fat![4] Larger muscles burn fat even when you're engaged in no activity due to the increased metabolic activity from strength training. Do we need any more reasons? Jeff Speakman states it best when he says, in effect, "you gotta have it!"

Program Characteristics

Now we're ready to talk about your actual program. To begin, you should plan on one hour sessions, three times per week. This provides enough stimulation (three times) and duration (one hour) to target basic exercises for the upper and lower body as well as the stabilizers (abdominals). The program will be periodized, of course, so this is only a beginning format.

Each session should begin with about five minutes of suppleness (warm-up) exercises. This increases your body temperature, promotes blood flow, and elasticity of the muscles. Moreover, each session should end with another five minutes of flexibility exercises. This is when you go for the really deep stretches. True flexibility concerns the joints, not the muscles, although the term is frequently associated with the muscles (technically, "suppleness" is the correct term for describing muscle elasticity). Flexibility is best performed after the workout, not before.

What to Exercise

In my research, I have determined that the following exercises constitute the minimum strength training requirements for martial artists. For the upper body: lat pull-downs, bent-over rows, one-arm dumbell curls, shoulder shrugs, and the upright row. For the lower body: squats, lunges, hamstring curls, and quadriceps exetensions. And for the stabilizers, crunches.

How to Exercise

As noted earlier, there is a lot of confusion about how much to lift and how many repetitions to perform. In part, the answer to this question depends on your personal objective. As outlined in Chapter Two, if you desire strength, choose a weight you can lift for three to six repetitions. If you want muscular endurance, choose a weight you can lift for 12 or more repetitions. If you want bodybuilding, choose a weight for eight to 10 repetitions.

However, don't start with any of these amounts right away if you previously haven't performed any strength training. In order to practice periodization (the science of systematic, planned progression), you should perform strength training in phases of four to six weeks each. The first phase is called transition and means that you'll lift light weights with high repetitions to begin conditioning your muscles. The second phase is hypertrophy (muscle mass) and that's when you begin using an amount of weight you can perform 12 repetitions with. The third phase is strength when you go for the six repetition sets. The fourth phase is power when you go for 15 repetitions at an accelerated tempo.

After a one to two week recovery period, you start the process all over again making adjustments for your increased strength. After a six month phased schedule like this, you then have the base to target your individual objective and so can concentrate on strength, endurance, or mass.

What Do the Sessions Look Like?

Now that you have a planned schedule and the exercises identified, let's review what an individual session looks like. After your suppleness exercises, begin the actual lifting. The amount of rest between sets depends, once again, on your objective. In the transition phase, your rest can be as short as 30 seconds. In hypertrophy, 60 seconds; and in strength, two minutes. The difference in duration is based on the intensity of the exercise and the time necessary to recover.

The amount of sets also depends on the phase of training. For instance:

PHASE	WEEKS	SETS / REPETITIONS	REST INTERVALS
Transition	4–6	2 sets of 25 reps each	30 seconds
Hypertrophy	4–6	3–4 sets of 8–12 reps each	60 seconds
Strength	4–6	5 sets of 6 reps each	2 minutes
Power	4–6	3 sets of 15 reps each	2 minutes
Rest	1–2	none or very light	

As a special time saving note, I personally work on my stabilizer muscles between sets of the strength workout. In other words, during the rest phase, I practice slow concentration kicks (or stretching) instead of just sitting around. Common sense dictates how this is done. I don't do squats and then slow roundhouse kicks; I do slow roundhouse kicks in the rest phases of upper body exercises. I stretch (splits, etc.) during the rest phase of the lower body exercises. I make my time count.

Other Considerations

For strength training to be effective, you must ensure adequate amounts of protein in your diet. Generally, one gram per pound of body weight will provide your muscles with the nutrition needed to incorporate the gains from strength training. Also, you might be curious about how long it will take to see gains from your program. Strength gains usually begin after four weeks of consistent training. Changes in size (increased muscle mass) normally take eight to 12 weeks to occur.

Can You Be Schwarzenegger?

One of the most pervasive myths concerning strength training concerns just how big you'll get. Can you get as big as Schwarzenegger if you use his pro-

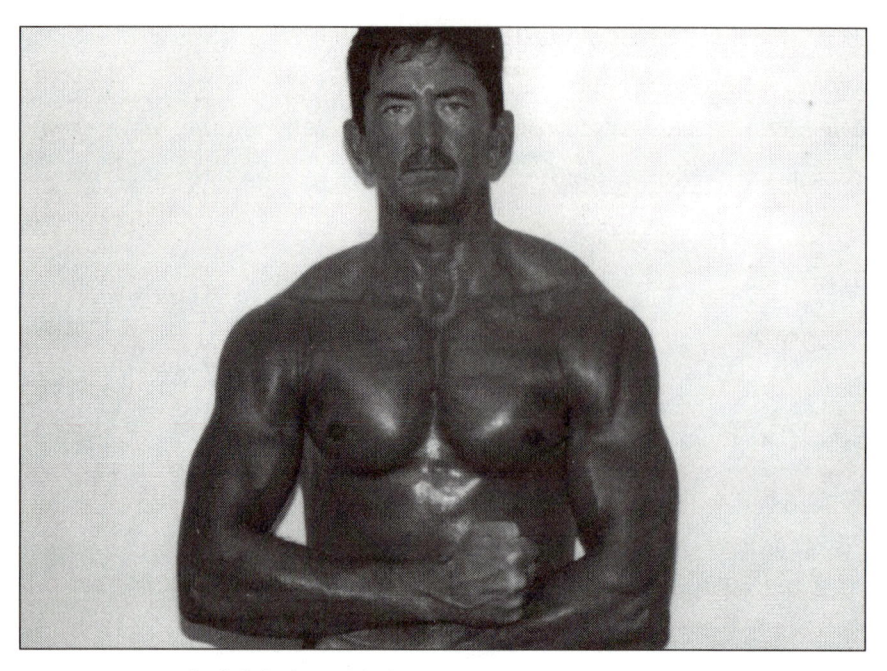

You may not get to look like Arnold, but you can improve your strength and physique.

gram or a similar program of an elite bodybuilder? Not necessarily. Ultimately, the potential for huge muscle mass rests in how many Type II muscle fibers you have (these are the white, fast twitch fibers found in sprinters as opposed to the red, slow twitch type found among endurance athletes).

Muscle Fiber Type

To test your potential for big mass in your legs or upper body, use the following no-cost assessments,[5] that you will see again in Chapter Five, with a slightly different application. For the lower body, use the quadriceps extension exercise, or, for the upper body, the bench press. In either case, you first have to determine what your one repetition maximum is. This may take a few tries and if a few attempts are necessary, wait five minutes between attempts to ensure you have rested muscles for these maximal efforts.

> **The potential for huge muscle mass rests in how many Type II muscle fibers you have.**

Once you have determined your one repetition maximum, take 70% of that amount and try to perform as many repetitions as possible. Based on the amount of repetitions you perform with that 70% of maximum, your fiber type can be approximated to be the following:

1–9	Fast twitch,	Type IIB (fewer repetitions = greater amount of Type II fibers)
10–11	Intermediate,	Type IIA
12 +	Slow twitch,	Type I (more fatigue resistant = able to do more repetitions)

The difference in fiber types directly impacts how big you'll get. If you have Type I, you won't get big but you can improve your performance by strengthening those muscles. If you have Type IIB, you can get big. If Type IIA, you'll get bigger, but not the type of proportions you see on Arnold.

Start Today!

Don't limit your maximize potential by failing to train for strength. You'll be better at your art, less prone to injury, and burn more fat than aerobic exercise. Superior athletes like Speakman and Van Damme are living examples that muscular size and flexibility are not incompatible.

Nutrition Matters

Sooner or later, it's bound to happen. Despite hard training and no missed workouts, you "bonked" at a recent tournament or during rigorous training. Without warning, you suddenly "ran out of gas" or felt puny, unable to go a minute longer. It may have felt like the "wall" that marathon runners describe. What happened?

> "What is enough for health is too little for pleasure"
> —St. Augustine

Core Needs

No matter the degree of dedication or discipline in training, maximum performance may elude you if core nutritional needs are not met. These needs concern what you eat, when you eat, and the amount of fluid required to sustain athletic prowess. Even if you're eating enough calories on a daily basis, there are certain practices that help avoid the "bonk" and maintain maximum performance, even if there is no deficiency in meeting the total daily caloric needs.

What You Eat

All human beings need a mixture of carbohydrates, proteins, and fat in their diet. The tricky part is in deciding what percentage of the diet should be devoted to these fundamentals of nutrition. In observations of myself and other athletes, I suspect that many athletes consume too much carbohydrates for two reasons. The first is the well-understood (but often misapplied) fact that carbohydrates are the main source of energy in high-intensity exercise. Secondly, many athletes (and the population in general) think that if they're eating "no-fat" foods, they will either lose weight or at least not gain weight. Both of these concepts need further explanation.

While carbohydrates are the primary fuel of high intensity exercise, if too many are consumed (or at the wrong time), protein needs are usually compromised. Protein is necessary to build strong muscles and in particular to repair the microscopic tears incurred in intense training. Furthermore, ingesting carbohydrates beyond actual daily caloric needs will make you fat! Excess calories are excess calories regardless of whether they are from carbohydrate, fat, or protein sources.

Current sport science opinion[6] suggests that if training lasts one-and-a-half hours per day, the percentages of consumption should be carbohydrate (60%), protein (15%), and fat (25%). If training lasts less than one-and-a-half hours per day, the percentages should be 51%, 17%, and 32%, respectively.

Generally speaking, carbohydrates are best derived from sources such as fresh fruits, vegetables, fruit juices, and plenty of grains (such as bread). Foods with "refined" carbohydrates (e.g., white rice) are second choice for top performance.

A martial athlete may consume a range of 3,500 to 4,000 calories per day depending on other daily activities. But that doesn't mean these calories are consumed at the right time to deliver them when needed. To illustrate this, let's assume you are maintaining a regular diet of appropriate carbohydrate, protein, and fat percentages. However, you have still experienced the occasional "bonk" and ran out of energy. How is that possible?

Glycogen Storage

When ingesting carbohydrates, a variety of complex processes occur in the body. One of the most important, in terms of athletic performance, is the conversion of carbohydrate into what is called "glycogen storage." While a certain amount of ingested carbohydrate is used to perform daily activities and exercise, remaining amounts are used to form a sort of "bank," or storage, that the body draws out during the demands of exercise, above 75% of maximum heart rate.

This storage capacity is trained and can be increased to a certain degree. Well-conditioned athletes can store up to two hours of glycogen. In other

Eating small amounts of carbohydrate rich foods after an event replenishes glycogen.

words, with an adequate consumption of carbohydrates and proper training, an athlete can sustain uninterrupted, elevated intensities of exercise (without additional eating) for up to two hours.

If the storage capacity is depleted, you may be able to continue exercising, but the intensity level will drop dramatically as the body switches from glycogen sources to fat sources. This switch is the "bonk." Fat stores are available in mass quantity but are capable of sustaining only moderate intensities of exercise, usually up to about 70% of maximum heart rate. As an energy source, fat is not capable of sustaining high intensity.

It's in the Timing

Many martial artists have experienced sudden depletion at a tournament or in rigorous training. The frustration is that many report proper diet habits and will report eating properly the actual day of competition. But many of these competitors won't eat anything following an early morning breakfast due to anxiety or a belief that they need to feel "light."

Yet consider the intensity and duration of training and competition. At a tournament, you may compete in forms in the morning, weapons around noon, and not begin sparring until the early afternoon. Since the glycogen storage capacity of even the most conditioned athletes is limited to around two hours, by 2:00 PM you may well feel unable to deliver even one more kick considering the energy used throughout day for warm-up, competing, and from anxiety.

One initial reaction to a "bonk" might be to train harder. But undertraining may not be the case at all. You may be well-trained but without the nutrients you need to maintain performance when you need them. Don't make matters worse by training even harder and further depleting yourself. Instead, consider these strategies.

Nutritional Strategy #1

Eat before you're hungry. Even with the most well-maintained diet, you need some small supplements of carbohydrate during the day of competition or rigorous training to maintain your energy levels and achieve maximum performance. The key is to anticipate your nutritional needs rather than waiting for the hunger trigger. There is a delay from the time you ingest food and when it becomes available for energy (the digestive process). So, waiting for the hunger trigger means that energy will not be available, at a minimum, for at least 30 minutes. If you're scheduled to fight at 2:00 pm, waiting until 1:45 pm to eat may cause more harm (e.g., gastric distress) than good.

Instead, ingest small amounts of carbohydrate approximately 60 minutes before a scheduled event to prevent depleting your glycogen storage during the event. Or, plan your nutrition systematically. After a good breakfast, create a schedule to ingest about 20 grams of carbohydrate per hour. This amount is small enough to avoid digestion problems but large enough to sustain performance.

The preferred form of carbohydrate ingestion prior to an event is energy drinks (such as Gatorade) since less digestion is required and therefore the energy can be quickly absorbed into the bloodstream and muscles. My personal favorite is two fig newtons (23 grams). This choice is inexpensive, stores well in an athletic bag, and helps meet the needs of tournament competition.

Nutritional Strategy #2

Eat soon after the event. Glycogen capacity, as the central source of athletic nutrition, is also largely influenced by when you eat after an event (or training). Sport scientists have identified a "glycogen window" that describes, in terms of time, how the human body absorbs and uses ingested carbohydrate most effectively. Athletic research demonstrates that carbohydrate is used to replenish your glycogen storage most effectively if consumed within two hours after exercising. If possible, eating within the first 30 minutes after exercise elicits the greatest restoration of this capacity.

Due to our culture and mindset, using this strategy can be difficult. Most of us are accustomed to a hard workout (or event) followed by some social talk, a shower, and eating several hours later. While this routine generates a great deal of personal satisfaction, it does not provide you with the greatest benefits available from carbohydrates to increase glycogen storage.

But, you can help meet the opportunities afforded by the "glycogen window" and follow our culture's exercise routine by employing some of the same concepts outlined in nutritional Strategy #1. Just as you used small amounts of carbohydrate in anticipation of an event, have some small amounts available afterward. By eating a banana or couple of fig newtons prior to showering, for example, you give the body some of what it needs to replenish itself at the time it is most capable of doing it (the glycogen window). But you'll still have an opportunity for more calories while relaxing with friends or family a couple of hours later. This strategy will also help prevent over-eating, a tendency induced by periods of prolonged deprivation.

Nutritional Strategy #3

Drink water like a fish! Even with great training and maximized glycogen storage, athletic performance requires a substantial amount of water. Water helps absorb nutrients, regulate temperature, carry oxygen, and a host of other functions. The general recommendation is to consume eight, eight-ounce glasses of water per day. But there is a better sign to determine proper hydration than following this general guideline.

Proper hydration before and after exercise ensures performance.

If your urine is yellow you are not drinking enough water. That's right. Colored urine means dehydration. When the body is adequately hydrated, urine will be clear as water. The one exception to this occurs when athletes take vitamin supplements. The excess water-soluble vitamins will be excreted through the urine and color it, although the body may be adequately hydrated. But in my experience as a coach and trainer, this is a very rare exception. Usually, if an athlete passes colored urine, that is a sure sign of dehydration.

What do you do? Drink water like a fish and keep drinking it until the urine becomes clear. This may take several hours after an event. But this simple litmus test of proper hydration is used by professional and amateur athletes alike to determine how much water they need.

Nutritional Strategy #4

Consider Creatine Monohydrate. During a high-intensity exercise like the martial arts, the primary energy source is carbohydrate. When a supramaximal effort is performed, such as a full-power roundhouse kick, a chemical process occurs in the powerful leg muscles. Stores of the energy source adenosine triphosphate (ATP) are broken down to release the energy needed to perform

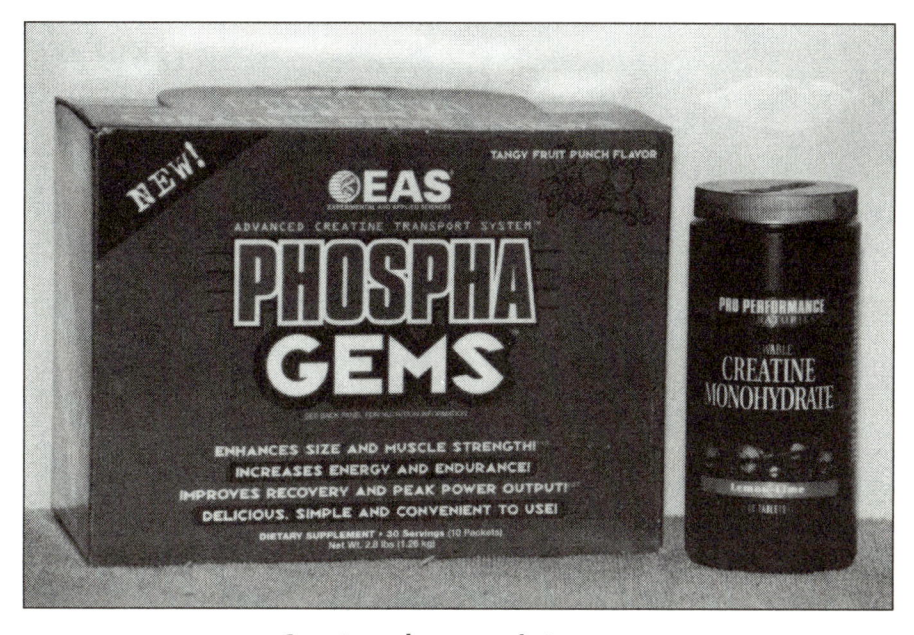

Creatine enhances explosive power.

the physical movement as we reviewed in Chapter One. A critical component of this ATP is a substance known as phosphocreatine.

When that high intensity kick is delivered, the phosphocreatine stores are somewhat depleted as the intramuscular process occurs. The human body is designed in such a way that the stores are resynthesized, or rebuilt, in order to perform subsequent physical activity.

The time it takes for these stores to replenish themselves can vary from perhaps 40 seconds up to three minutes depending on the extent and duration of the activity as well as the amount of creatine available. If the stores are "full" and well-trained, this resynthesis process occurs more rapidly than in untrained athletes.

In order to both increase the ATP stores and expedite the resynthesis process, sport researchers have clinically demonstrated that using creatine monohydrate delays muscle fatigue and enhances resynthesis. Several researchers have determined that ingesting creatine monohydrate increases the total creatine content in muscles by an average of 20 to 30%. This means that athletes with this increased capacity can last longer and recover faster than those without this aid.

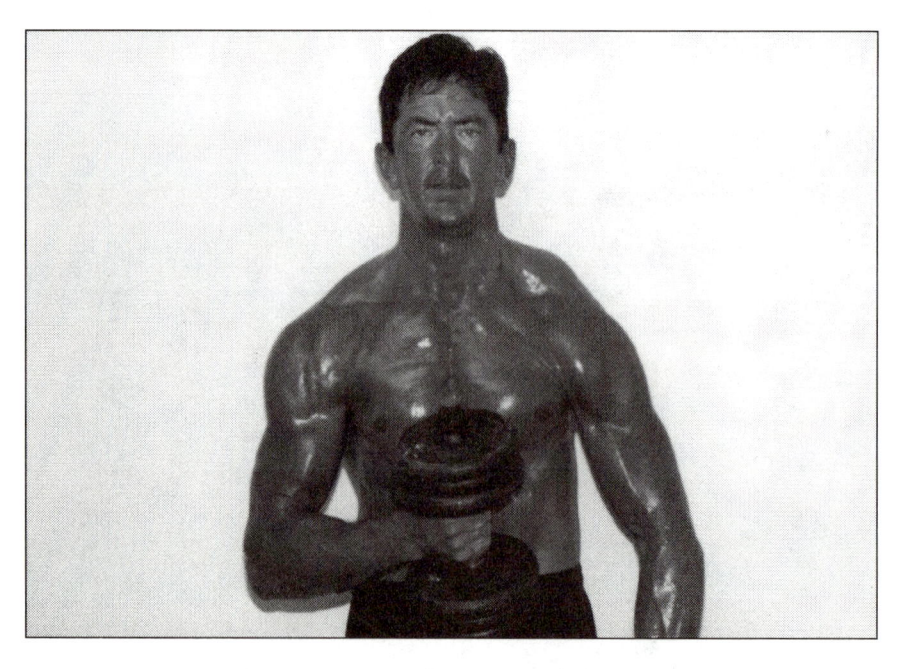

Creatine increased my strength by 23%

Here's How It Worked For Me

I reviewed the research[7] on using this supplement and determined the consensus was to ingest 20–25 grams for five to six days (known as the "load" phase) followed by an average daily dosage of 2.5 grams (known as the "maintenance" phase).

Before I began the load phase, I performed a baseline assessment of six strength exercises (using weights) and two endurance exercises (push-ups and pull-ups). It is important to note here that I had begun my strength training program about two months before the assessment so there was a definite foundation for this experiment.

My Subjective Assessment

On the very first day I began creatine loading, I sensed an increased ability to perform during my muscle endurance exercises of push-ups and pull-ups. But, to keep my scheduled reassessment pure, I didn't try to "max out." I kept performing designated sets with prescribed recovery times. It's difficult to describe, but I simply didn't feel the same sense of despair on the pull-up bar. If you're like me, after you knock out the first five or so repetitions, you have to fight to get the rest. And, it can feel like the reps will end at any second due to muscle fatigue.

Using creatine, I felt stronger and more confident. I sensed I was in control of the exercise. I felt the same thing when using weights for the strength training.

My Objective Assessment

After a two week period, one for loading and one for maintenance, I performed the same strength and endurance assessment I did prior to use of creatine monohydrate. The results?

Phenomenal.

My strength with weights increased a mean of 23% among four multi-joint exercises (e.g., upright row). My endurance in the push-up and pull-up category increased a mean of 31%. For a reason I don't understand, I didn't see an increase in the single-joint exercises (e.g., biceps curl). I also experienced positive changes in my physique due to the two week usage of this valuable supplement.

Although I gained three pounds (presumably from the increased metabolic activity and water retention), I lost an inch from my waist. And, I gained in the right places! The diameter of my biceps increased a quarter of an inch, my quadriceps increased half of an inch, and my chest a full inch! I feel and look stronger!

Now, don't get me wrong. I raced bicycles for a decade and have a high proportion of Type I muscle fibers (the type that don't lead to the VanDamme physique). So I'm not saying that creatine can enable you to overcome your general genetic disposition. But it can certainly improve it. I'm living proof.

So, How About You?

My experience, along with the clinical research performed to date, strongly suggests that you should consider this supplement. Improved muscle strength and endurance is important for any martial artist, whether the activity is karate, judo, or ju-jitsu. If maximal muscle intensity is involved, this supplement can help.

I must emphasize that you can't simply ingest this supplement without a base of strength training or without performing strength training concurrent with the supplement's loading and maintenance phase. Remember, I had begun my weight training two months prior to the experiment and have performed strength training (in varying degrees) for several years.

What About This "Zone" Thing?

There's quite a bit of debate about the role of carbohydrates due to Dr. Barry Sears book, *The Zone*.[8] In fact, author June Castro of "Breaking the High-Carb Myth" (Inside Kung-Fu, March 1997), offers some necessary reevaluation of the role of carbohydrates in the martial artist's diet. However, there are several assumptions in the article that do not reflect accepted sport science for martial artists. Let's spend a few moments to dispel that confusion.

Dr. Sears states there is a ". . . misconception that carbohydrates provide the body with energy. In fact, the number-one source for energy is not carbohydrates: it's fat." This statement is only true insofar as it relates to sedentary activities and low intensity levels of exercise. Instead, sport scientists such as David Costill of the Human Performance Research Laboratory have demonstrated that the use of fat alone can sustain exercise only up to levels of about 70% of maximum heart rate (MHR).

As previously stated, while there is still some minimal utilization of fats beyond 70% and up to 95% of MHR, "explosive power" athletes such as martial artists, wrestlers, and football players actually use stored glycogen (from ingested carbohydrates) in the muscles to fuel high-intensity exercise at elevated heart rates above 70% of MHR. This is particularly true in performance that involves the Type IIB (fast twitch) muscle fibers. Carbohydrates are not a mere "secondary" source of energy as stated by Dr. Sears but are the very fuel of our high intensity efforts.

Even with adequate carbohydrate intake, after three successive days of hard training glycogen levels in the muscle may remain only 75% full on a diet with 70% carbohydrate.

Thus, statements such as "eating a high-carb diet doesn't give you energy" and "a high carb diet will inevitably work against you" are not substantiated in applied sport science and must be understood in the context that carbohydrate is the primary source of energy at intensities above 70% of MHR.

It cannot be overemphasized, then, that martial artists must ensure a diet with appropriate levels of carbohydrate in order to maintain adequate levels of muscle glycogen. Even with adequate carbohydrate intake, after three successive days of hard training glycogen levels in the muscle may remain only 75% percent full on a diet with 70% carbohydrate. (Due to the effects of high-intensity training and the recuperation and muscle glycogen resynthesis that attend it, 100% capacity in successive days of hard training is impossible). This 75% capacity is a "best case" scenario. In a "worst case" scenario, levels can fall to 25% on a diet of only 40% carbohydrate. And, because well-trained muscles can only store up to two hours worth of glycogen, this means that on the third day of successive hard training, a martial artist may falter after only 30 minutes of continuous, intense exercise.

"The Zone" also contains the idea that consuming a high-carb meal causes drastic fluctuations in the blood sugar level and may cause hypoglycemia due to elevated levels of insulin. This is partially true (in an acute sense) but the concerns can be addressed without neglecting needed carbohydrates for high intensity training. Simply use the recommended daily percentages based on the amount of training time outlined in the "What You Eat" section of this chapter.

These guidelines guard against the consumption of unnecessary carbohydrates (which can lead to increased body fat). These guidelines should also be considered against Dr. Sear's suggestion to use pasta (carbohydrate) as a "side dish" and eat proteins as a main dish.

It is critical to ensure adequate levels of carbohydrate are consumed prior to, during, and after periods of exercise. This is because failure to maintain liver glycogen levels during exercise will cause blood glucose levels to fall. Since the brain depends on an adequate glucose supply, falling glucose levels (hypoglycemia) may ultimately lead to exhaustion due to impaired brain functioning. (Ever wonder why Chuck Norris carries around those Snickers bars?)

The Role of Insulin

Interest in "The Zone" approach has partially been triggered by concerns about the presence of insulin triggered by carbohydrate ingestion. Again, this is partially true. But the critical issue is the amount of ingested carbohydrate and the subsequent volume of insulin produced.

If exercise starts with moderate levels of elevated insulin, there is an increased utilization of muscle glycogen—that nutrient that fuels high-intensity exercise among the fast twitch muscle fibers. The key is to have a moderate amount such as what would be activated by the 25 gram per hour recommendation. Hypoglycemia can occur with too much insulin or with too little blood sugar, particularly as it relates to the liver.

Dr. Sears also states that the muscle cells and brain compete for glycogen.

Moderate amounts of carbohydrate, like fig newtons, maintain blood sugar levels without triggering excessive insulin.

In fact, ingested glucose (carbohydrate) may be utilized by either the liver (which supplies the brain) or muscles, or a combination of both depending on the respective "needs of the moment" regarding storage and activity. If glycogen stores in the muscles are reduced (e.g., from training), a large percentage of ingested glucose will be diverted to replenish those stores accordingly. But the body is designed to ensure that glucose needs of the brain, kidney, and red blood cells are met as well.

Furthermore, once the liver and muscle glycogen stores are filled, any excess carbohydrate is stored as triglycerides (fat) in the adipose tissue. However, in numerous research biopsies, little of the triglyceride fat stored in adipose tissue comes from carbohydrate. In practice, almost all is derived from ingested fat.

To summarize, martial artists may not expect fats to fuel their high intensity exercise and so the question of how the body can access fatty acids and not glycogen does not apply. The bottom line is that martial artists should be cautious about "The Zone" approach. Instead, martial artists must ensure a proportionate and moderate amount of carbohydrates is consumed to create an adequate storage of liver and muscle glycogen for high intensity exercise.

Athletes have mistakingly believed that ingestion of a high-carbohydrate diet is the complete answer to high performance nutrition needs. In an acute sense, this has led to the disproportionate consumption of excessive carbohydrates immediately prior to an event (the spaghetti dinner) that does trigger excessive insulin. This results in the "sleepy" response as well as impaired utilization and should be avoided.

In a more general sense, the over-emphasis and misapplication of carbohydrate strategies often leads to a deficiency regarding ingestion of adequate proteins to rebuild and strengthen muscular strength needs. However, not recognizing that carbohydrates are the primary source of high-intensity exercise, and therefore maintaining adequate glycogen storage, is a proven culprit of impaired performance.

Nutrition Summary

Proper nutrition is like balancing a checkbook. To offset withdrawals, timely deposits are needed. The martial arts are rigorous and require significant withdrawals from your available energy stores. You make timely deposits by eating small amounts of carbohydrates before you're hungry and by recognizing the glycogen window that follows exercise. And, the sensation of thirst is not an accurate indicator of the body's need for water. We must drink water aggressively.

Some social critics have noted that man is the only animal that eats when he is not hungry. But a successful athlete eats before he is hungry so that he doesn't experience the "bonk."

CHAPTER FOUR

THE TOTAL QUALITY PERFORMANCE LOG

"Every lofty idea eventually degenerates into work."
—PETER DRUCKER

No training plan is really complete without a system of measurement. Successful athletes use measurement to determine the effectiveness of their training (and decide what success is!). Bruce Lee used measurement in his training plans. Look at the photographs of his "exercise list" and "body improvement list" in *The Bruce Lee Story*.[1] The exercise list states what he would do, the improvement list demonstrated the results. This is the very core of TQM: planning, measuring, and analysis. In Total Quality Martial Arts, you'll do just as Bruce Lee did: you'll plan and analyze your training. In this chapter, we'll look at the TQM method of accomplishing this end.

In my review of existing martial art publications, I found only one book that even attempted to record and evaluate training, Dr. Art Brisacherit's *Maximize Your Martial Arts Training*.[2] In his book, Dr. Brisacher measures progress among exercise variables such as running, push-ups, sparring, and forms but does not consider the variables that affect performance. What you will learn in this chapter will enable you to specifically identify what contributes to your personal success. It's the Total Quality way.

Perhaps the most pressing issue involved in measurement is what standard is to be used. The founder of TQM measured how well his crops grew to determine effectiveness. That meant looking at the process as well as the result. You might naturally think your measurement of effectiveness should be "winning." But there are more relevant, and "gracious," standards to use. As I demonstrated in Chapter One, success does not justify training methods and you should not necessarily decide, for instance, that resistance training is effective by how well you do at the next tournament.

Winning is Not the Only Measurement

Winning is a relative matter. It doesn't necessarily mean the best athlete wins. It means that one person finishes first on a particular day under favorable circumstances. While you might win a local tournament that doesn't necessarily mean that you're the best martial artist in the city. What about the person who might have beat you who didn't compete in that specific tournament because of a conflicting commitment? What about the person who you know has beat you in sparring but could not enter the tournament because it was a closed tournament (e.g., only certain styles permitted to enter)? Or how about the time you lost because a judge missed seeing your technique? Someone else won the trophy but you were better, the victim of judging.

These are but just a few examples of many that indicate winning is a relative and ever-changing phenomenon that usually rests on one person for only a very short period of time. Sure, we all like to win a trophy. But that act is not meant to validate our training or serve as a the exclusive means of measurement. Winning is a temporary reward for hard work and usually good fortune. Furthermore, if we are seeking certain martial art goals such as unity with another person, words like "victory" or "defeat" are meaningless: the real key is coexisting with your opponent.[3]

Some martial artists suggest that the only true victory regards our own spirituality, which we'll address to a degree in Part Two. In fact, revered aikido master Kochi Tohei states that "if we fail to win over ourselves, even though we win over others, we are doing nothing but satisfying our own conceit and vanity. If, on the other hand, we do win over ourselves, we have no need to win over any other person. . . . A relative victory is fragile, but a victory over oneself is absolute."[4] And, as Tohei further observes, it may be difficult to maintain the spiritual condition sought through martial art practice if all year you keep your spirit in turmoil over matches and contests.

Besides its subjective and relative nature, the single-minded pursuit of a "win" can distort our perception. Retired Chicago Bulls coach Phil Jackson points out that in true spirituality, everything is sacred, even the enemy (or opponent).[5] And he is not saying this just because he was on top of the NBA: he has played and coached with losing and winning teams. Jackson further states that in our athletic pursuits we must use an approach that honors the humanity of both sides while recognizing that only one victor can emerge. "As strange as it may seem," he writes, "being able to accept . . . defeat with equanimity gives you the freedom to go out on the floor and give the game your all."

As an alternative approach to that relative standard of winning and the distortions it can cause, a Total Quality Martial Artist can base his or her measurement on an objective standard. As an example, consider a professional football team. During a game a particular team may accumulate some pretty impressive statistics—most yards gained, fewest yards allowed, greatest time of possession. But at the end of the game, the opponent scores two quick touchdowns on errors and "wins" the game. That relative standard, winning the game, doesn't tell the true story. It overlooks the statistics and how one team actually outplayed the other. In turn, a team can feel good about its effort, even in "losing," if an objective standard is used to measure their performance. Perhaps by gaining more yards, allowing fewer yards, and increasing the time of possession the team increased their previous statistics in those categories by 25%! That's improvement! And what's more, it is objective. It also says more about the long-term prospects and depth of the "losing" team than a "fluke" win by the outplayed opponent.

> It may be difficult to maintain the spiritual condition sought through martial art practice if all year you keep your spirit in turmoil over matches and contests.

As notable *aikidoist* George Leonard states, sometimes we may have to surrender a certain amount of competency (the elusive win) to gain a "higher competence" in the form of continuous improvement.[6] George uses the analogy of a golfer who routinely shoots in the 80s but wants to be in the 70s.

One strategy could be to focus down, try even harder, and desperately pursue that lower score. But that only uses the skills already possessed and seeks to apply them more arduously. This is limiting because it means trying to achieve higher levels of competence with the same consciousness.

A second strategy could be to "let go" a little and learn new skills. This might mean experimenting with some different shots or using different clubs—things that might temporarily send scores into the 90s until the discovery of what works. Then, with that new knowledge, trying for the 70s. The irony bears emphasis. As long as someone keeps using the same techniques that achieve the 80s, those techniques will keep them in the 80s. Those techniques have to be "let go" to see a positive change. Sort of like the Zen teaching to "empty your cup." The Total Quality Performance Log enables you to experiment, find out what works for you, and achieve a "higher competency."

You see, measurement is a sword that cuts in many directions. If it's based on a objective standard and separated from "winning," then we can put forth our best effort and recognize progress or improvement. Our reward comes from objectively improving our performance, like that professional football team. In terms of martial art, perhaps this is measured by not allowing a certain technique to score against us. Or in training, we increase our vertical jump by two inches which means more effective jumping techniques in competition. But if we're wrapped up in winning as a measurement of our efforts, then we're overlooking the objective standards that give us meaningful feedback about our training.

Creating the Total Quality Training Log

A Total Quality Training Log is an instrument that enables you to measure your performance against relative or objective measurements, or both. A relative measurement, again, might be your competitive record. An objective measurement would mean seeing how well you do against established standards. For example, you could use a book such as *Training Theory for Martial Arts*[7] by

PHYSICAL CONSIDERATIONS

Tony Gummerson to determine how many push-ups it takes to have a good performance. Or, you could measure yourself against the standards set by elite kickboxers that I'll review in Chapter Five.

At an absolute minimum, you should analyze your training to measure performance and therefore modify your training as needed to ensure improvements—like Bruce Lee did. In Total Quality Martial Arts you can accomplish this by use of the "comparative" and "sequential" methods of recording your training, which, when combined together, form the Total Quality Training Log. Let's review the steps involved in creating this unique instrument.

Comparative Performance Indicators

Remember in Chapter Two that you performed a volume baseline assessment of the total annual hours spent training. Now you will conduct a performance baseline describing indicators of athletic ability that affect both the practice of your martial art and general fitness level. Once you conduct the performance baseline, you reassess yourself at periodic intervals, such as every 30 days, to measure improvement. Among other things, this type of comparative monitoring lets you know if you are overtraining (expressed as decreased performance), or undertraining (seen in no improvements). In the following example, our Total Quality martial artist has performed a self-assessment test on the first day of every month for 10 months (see table on page 74). Some of the tests are self-explanatory, such as how many push-ups can be performed. Others, such as the vertical jump and the three minute step test, would require some research and adoption of standards, such as those outlined by Tony Gummerson, to determine how the test(s) should be performed.

With recorded information like this, there is a wealth of insight you can glean about your training program. For example, look at the waking pulse of this athlete's log across the 10 months. Overall, it hasn't decreased from the aerobic training performed but that's not necessarily a problem for this athlete. With a pulse in the 50s, he is in good shape anyway. It is interesting to note, however, that his pulse was higher on January 1st (61) after a night of limited sleep. Since pulse rate is an indication of recovery, this athlete now knows to be careful before critical training or competitive events.

Comparative Log Measurements

MONTH/DAY	8/1	9/1	10/1	11/1	12/1	1/1	2/1	3/1	4/1	5/1
Sleep	8	7	8	6	6	5	8	7	7	8
Pulse	52	54	55	55	55	61	54	55	55	54
Weight	165	165	164	165	168	170	168	165	163	163
Push-ups	50	52	54	54	54	54	56	60	62	65
Pull-ups	12	12	13	12	12	13	12	13	13	12
Sit-ups	80	82	85	86	86	86	88	90	92	95
Vert. jump	23	23	23	23	22	22	23	23	23	23
3 min. step	110	110	108	107	108	110	108	105	103	102
Hamstring	12.5	12.5	13	13	13.5	13.5	14	14	14	14

DIAMETER

Biceps	14	14	14.25	14.25	14.25	14	14.25	14.50	14.75	15
Forearm	11	11	11	11	11	11	11	11	11	11
Quadriceps	19	19	19	19	19	19	19	19	19	19
Calves	13	13.5	13.5	13.5	13.5	13.5	13.75	13.75	13.75	13.75
Waist	33	32.5	32.5	32.5	33	33	32.5	32	32	32

Next, look at his weight. Overall, he lost a couple of pounds through training but nothing noteworthy. But again, look at his higher weights on 12/1 and 1/1, both following holidays: he gained some there. Is this something to be concerned about if overall he lost a couple of pounds between August and May? Possibly. Look down at the vertical jump and note that his only decreases were at those points. If this athlete had a critical event during this time, the holiday overeating may well have impaired his performance.

Jointly reviewing training records pinpoints weaknesses and promotes continuous improvement.

Now those are some isolated incidents in this comparative log. But there are also some systematic, or lasting, occurrences that are very noteworthy. For instance, look at the ability to perform push-ups and sit-ups. Averaged together, his increases in these performance indicators represent a 20% increase in local muscular endurance! That's great! This means the athlete is doing something right. And if these were your results, you could look back at the training plan you were using during that time and enter a big star by that portion of the plan because it worked!

On the other hand, look at the pull-ups: no improvement. How could this athlete improve in push-ups but not pull-ups? As mentioned in Chapter One it's a matter of training specificity. By cross-referencing this comparative log with the training plan used, you could possibly learn that you didn't incorporate the right exercises to improve pull-up ability (such as lat pull-downs and upright rowing).

Do you see how this use of the comparative log can be beneficial? It allows you to objectively assess your training methods and the results. Let's look at a few more examples.

This athlete's log also features diameter measurements of several body parts. Note that the biceps have increased (probably from the push-ups) as well as the calves (probably from rope jumping) and the waist has decreased by an inch. Considering that a couple of pounds were lost, this means the athletic appearance has been improved and probably means a change in the body fat percentage. These are good signs to reinforce those aspects of the training program.

Yet the quadriceps did not increase at all. Like the push-up/pull-up discrepancy, this means the training plan is not yet complete. The calves increased but apparently not enough exercises were used to stimulate the quadriceps (such as squats and lunges). If increased quadriceps diameter is desired, then the training plan, after reviewing this comparative log, must be adjusted.

As you can see, it is evident that the comparative log can make the difference in reaching your goals or receiving no investment for your training. By cross-referencing it with the training plan you will know what works for you and what doesn't. If you wanted bigger quadriceps and used some plan you read about in a magazine (but had no improvements in 10 months), it's time to abandon that plan—regardless of whether it worked for someone else. You see, once again, that success doesn't justify training methods.

By use of the comparative log in my own training, I have determined a negative relationship between endurance swimming and my ability to perform push-ups. Likewise, a certain amount of bicycling has detrimental effects on my kicking height, due to the shortening of the hip flexors. I have determined a positive relationship between kicking power and running sprints up to a distance of 440 yards (not actually a sprint at that distance). You too can find these things out about yourself by maintaining a Total Quality Performance Log and measuring the results of training.

You should create your own standards to create your comparative log. For instance, there are various types of electronic measuring equipment to measure hand strength, reaction speed, and quickness. These create objective standards and reference points for you to improve upon and measure your (hopefully improved) performance. The comparative log is your tool to measure your performance for your individual objectives.

The Sequential Training Log

Along with the comparative section of the Total Quality Training Log that is used on a periodic basis, there is a great reward in maintaining a "sequential" section that records your training on a daily basis. For instance, when noting a high performance on the comparative log, you can reference the sequential log and see what factors in the weeks leading to the test may have contributed to that high performance, just as you cross-referenced the training plan.

Although you can create a log in any matter that suits your individual needs, including a hand-written or electronic type, here is an example to illustrate the principle of the Sequential Training Log.

Week: 8/1/96							Avg/Total
SLP 8	SLP 7	SLP 8	SLP 6	SLP 3	SLP 8	SLP 8	6.8 (48)
PUL 52	PUL 50	PUL 50	PUL 54	PUL 58	PUL 52	PUL 52	52.5
WT 165	WT 165	WT 166	WT 166	WT 167	WT 166	WT 165	165.7
TOT 2.0	TOT 1.5	TOT 2.3	TOT 1.4	TOT 1.0	TOT 2.0	TOT-	11.0
TYP MA Bag	TYP Run Wts	TYP Run Bag	STYP MA Wts	TYP STR Abs	TYP MA Bike	TYP-	

The abbreviations in this sequential log stand for "SLP" (sleep), "PUL" (pulse), "WT" (weight), "TOT" (total exercise time), and "TYPE" (types of physical activity performed, including non-training such as household chores). This information can be used for measurement and analysis just like the comparative log. Let's review several examples.

As we did with the comparative log, let's look at the pulse. One great result of recording the waking pulse on a daily basis is that it creates a standard to judge your recovery level. After you've recorded it for a week, as in this sequential log, you determine that your pulse is an average of approximately 52 beats per minute (that's good). In sport science, an elevated pulse (10 additional beats per minute) means that you are either ill or have not recovered from the previous day's training. In other words, knowing that your average pulse is 52 means that if you awaken to 62 to or more, you must adjust your training plan. You can't go as hard or you risk injury or further illness. On the particular week of this sequential log, our athlete only received three hours sleep on the fifth day, experienced a slight pulse increase, and so curtailed training to only an hour of stretching and abdominal work for that day. The next day the pulse dropped back to 52 so the proper modification was made.

This sequential log can therefore be used to develop an accurate baseline for the average amount of sleep on a daily and weekly basis, weight, total work out time, and, of course, the pulse. These factors help you determine what is right (or wrong) about your training.

You should, of course, modify this sequential log to reflect how you organize and perform your training. For example, you may want to record a precise description of the workout under "TYP" (type), such as "three, five minute rounds on heavybag." But if you closely follow your overall training plan, this may not be necessary—you would only need to reference the plan for a fuller description of the workout.

Further Uses of Training Logs

There are all sorts of information that you can record to create your Total Quality Performance Log. It's up to your imagination and needs. My log includes an injury notebook wherein I record how certain injuries occurred, the duration of healing, and treatments used. This enables me to share helpful hints with other athletes and means I don't have to conduct research on certain topics more than once in the event of repeat injuries.

You should also consider a log that documents what techniques you successfully use in sparring or competition so that you can use them again. Don't trust your memory on this one! Write it down for future reference. I have also found that use of a hand-held voice recorder cassette is very useful after attending tournaments or seminars. While driving home, I record my thoughts and memories while they're fresh for future use and modifying my training. This also serves as a sort of "comparative" log, especially after tournament events.

An Example from the Police

Starting in 1988, the Los Angeles Police Department (LAPD) began a Total Quality-like process that has revolutionized their physical training.[8] In the true spirit of conducting research, recording information, and measuring results, the LAPD analyzed use-of-force reports to identify a set of patterns that occurred during arrests. Through this process, they were able to determine which arrest techniques were being used by both criminals and by the police—and which ones worked. Once the LAPD determined that 63% of confrontations ended up on the ground, they began incorporating grappling training for their officers.

It is that type of specificity and measurement that is needed to make our training effective. If the LAPD only relied on a more generalized, logical approach, they might have surmised that officers simply need exceptional arm strength for putting on the cuffs. But before the cuffs comes a lot of wrestling—the type grappling will help with. In effect, their careful research and measurement creates a Total Quality process.

How to Use the Star's Training Programs

You are now armed with some vital core principles of sport science and the ability to intelligently design and measure your training. This provides you with a means to interpret the things you read in magazines and hear your favorite martial artist discuss regarding training. So, what do you do with the next "star" training program you encounter? Based on the principles outlined in the Total Quality Martial Arts approach, there are three essential questions to answer.

1. Does it conflict with sport science? If someone says they lift light weights in order to increase their strength, you know this is wrong. Light weights used with more than 12 repetitions creates local muscular endurance, not strength.

If the advice conflicts with sport science, disregard. If it matches, proceed to question two.

2. Is it appropriate to your goal? If a "star" claims to run five miles a day, that's great. But does it accomplish your objectives? If your goal is to win at point karate, that type of endurance training is not only unnecessary but inappropriate. Remember, glycolytic (fast twitch) enzymes are sacrificed for the oxidative type (see Chapter Two). Again, if the advice is incongruent with your goal, disregard it. If it matches, proceed to question three.

3. Does it require an incremental approach? This is perhaps the most crucial question of all. Assuming the training advice meets the criteria outlined in questions one and two above, it may call for you to perform considerably above your current capacity. For example, plyometrics are an excellent means of training for martial artists, sound in science, and probably applicable to your objectives. But before starting them, there are certain guidelines to meet such as the ability to squat 1.5 times your weight and four to six weeks of prior resistance training. If you simply jump in to plyometric training without regard to these types of considerations, you may become injured.

Some research will be necessary first. Generally, if you invest in thoroughly answering these questions, you are equipped to determine whether a "star's" program is right for you.

Reviewing the Total Quality Martial Art Process

At this point, we have now covered the framework of the Total Quality Martial Arts approach. As indicated in Chapter One, it all begins with an ongoing review of sport science. You simply cannot hope to excel in your martial art without an understanding of the energy systems and muscle fibers needed for your activity. Otherwise, you could spend a lot of wasted time on training approaches that are not only of no help to your endeavor but actually impair it (such as excessive endurance training). On the basis of sport science, you then create an annual training plan with distinct periods that allow you to see improvements, ensure recovery, and peak for certain events. However, it is no good to simply train, even if based on sport science, without realizing the individualized effects of that plan. That's why you need measurement such as that afforded by the Total Quality Performance Log. Obviously, you don't have to use all of the performance indicators I've listed as an example in this chapter. You can personalize your log to reflect the needs of your pursuit. But in principle, effective measurement means that you need a comparative and sequential log to cross-reference with the training plan and sport science in order to fully adopt the Total Quality approach.

As we review this overall process (sport science, training plan, training log) you're probably getting the picture that you need a pretty big notebook to make this effort work. Probably even several notebooks. No, this approach is not as simple as putting on your uniform and following the class routine. Neither is it as simple as reading a magazine article and adopting the routine outlined by your favorite star.

A vulnerability that we all must guard against is the tendency to see life, and particularly our martial art, as a static process. In other words, that if we study enough, we will gain all the knowledge there is to know of a subject, such as training, and then we'll simply live and teach it. This illusion is attractive because it simultaneously appeals to our sense of security, competency, and recognition. That's probably a primary reason for the emphasis on "traditional" martial arts that resists "modernization." But to say that a style has not changed for centuries is about stagnation,[9] not reality.

Knowledge and life are in constant change. They are very dynamic. What we knew about sport science decades ago changes as the laboratories reveal more about the human body. That's why the TQM precept of *kaizen*, or continuous improvement, is so important. We may well have a good picture of how training should be performed at this particular point in the evolution of science. But in 10 years we may have to abandon it due to new revelations. That can be exciting for some and depressing for others.

To practice *kaizen* and Total Quality Martial Arts you should have a notebook full of materials. When you see an article about someone's training routine, put it in your notebook and then begin researching whether it represents sound science and will help you achieve your goal. Keep your training plans and logs together so that you can compare them year to year. Then, throughout the process (which never ends in a Total Quality approach), invest in yourself by studying the literature available through organizations such as the International Sport Sciences Association and National Strength and Conditioning Association (references are in the Appendix). These types of organizations provide you with the research performed by specialists in the field and laboratories throughout the world.

I was over 30 years old before I learned about sport science and the Total Quality approach. Before that time, I only listened to coaches and tried to adopt the recommendations of elite athletes. But once I learned how to integrate these two aspects I helped myself and numerous other athletes achieve quantifiable progress and avoid unnecessary injuries, overtraining, and burnout. As you practice the principles of Total Quality Martial Arts, you will receive those same rewards. Again, it's not as easy as the ritualistic method, but it's intelligent, personalized, and effective. That's what our training, and lives, are all about.

PART TWO

Spiritual Components

INTRODUCTION

*"In my neighborhood, every
adult is a dead child."*
—Joseph Lyford

It is important from the onset to clarify what is meant by the term "spiritual." The use of this term is not necessarily synonymous with "religious," but, according to the individual, it may well incorporate that aspect. According to Scott Peck, to be spiritual means to "live in accordance with an unseen order of things." Religious people believe that "unseen" order to be God. I call this "theistic" spirituality. (Theistic means a personal God). Others, especially from the Eastern mindset, see an impersonal order of things, sometimes referred to as the "Tao." This is the general meaning of the term spiritual in martial arts, although Western practioneers often equate "spirituality" with the ability to endure strenuous physical training.

But to embrace true spirituality I admire the question posed by Herman Kauz who asks: "If studying the martial arts for a number of years is supposed to effect salutory changes in us on the levels of mind and spirit as well as on the physical level, do our actions in everyday life reflect the these changes?"[1] Can we consider ourselves or our art "spiritual" if it doesn't affect our work and relationships? These must be included if we will be both fully human and capable of top performance as martial athletes. Do you really believe that you can consistently perform to your potential if your mind is distracted by unresolved issues at work or home?

In his best-selling book, *The Road Less Traveled*,[2] Scott Peck addresses avocations (something we don't do for our livelihood, like nonprofessional martial artists). By intention, he points out, avocations are to be self-nurturing activities. They serve as a means of self-renewal that energize a person in his or her other daily activities.

But, Peck writes, if an avocation becomes an end in itself, then it becomes a substitute for, rather than a means to, self-development. Peck illustrates this with an example of retired men and women whose primary goal in life is to shave a few more strokes off their golf game. "This dedicated effort to improve their skill serves to give them a sense of progress in life and thereby assists them in ignoring the reality that they have actually stopped progressing, having given up the effort to improve themselves as human beings. If they loved themselves more they would not allow themselves to passionately settle for such a shallow goal and narrow future."[3]

There may be a tendency to laugh about the retired golfers. But sadly, far too many athletes, including martial artists, have also unconsciously embraced the goal of improved performance to the detriment of becoming

Technical proficiency doesn't inherently mean spiritual fitness.

SPIRITUAL COMPONENTS

fully human.

To be fully human, an athlete must do more in action and attitude than merely tolerate life's activities while waiting for the next training session or competitive event. To become a fully developed self, a martial athlete must establish an internal spiritual harmony that expresses itself in the core dimensions of work and relationships. This is Total Quality Martial Arts.

You may be in the process of developing an exceptional cardiovascular system, superb muscle tone, and winning technique. But if a basic spiritual congruence and level of mutual satisfaction is not maintained in the core dimensions of your life (e.g., work and relationships), the stain will eventually show up in your training, personal life, or both. The athletes of many sports unfortunately provide very sad examples.

Remember the basketball great Lynn Bias? Dead from an overdose of cocaine. How about Magic Johnson? His off-court behavior led him to contract the AIDS virus. Or how about Micky Mantle, one of baseball's premier hall of famers. Unbelievably, even throughout Mantle's stellar career he was an alcoholic, a problem which began at age 19. Not until the age of 62 did Mantle finally submit himself for treatment after a 43 year struggle with the disease. And, in my own city there are a core of approximately one dozen professional football players who are mentioned in the civil disturbance section as well as the sports section of the newspaper. Clearly, internal spiritual chaos can lead not only to diminished performance but endanger your general welfare as well.

But what, you may say, do these examples have to do with my life as a martial artist? These examples are important illustrations for more than one reason. Primarily, they demonstrate the need for both a physical and spiritual emphasis in our lives as martial athletes. But even more poignantly, these examples destroy a myth that many of us carry. How many times have you thought within yourself that everything would be great if you could just win a tournament or consistently maintain a certain training program? I've thought this. But these tragic examples of professional athletes show that an athlete does not automatically become satisfied once a certain level of achievement is attained. Many athletes believe that all will be well once the "crown" is received. These lives tell a different story. "Wise men eventually realize that none of the wealth, fame, power, or acclaim that they have acquired actually gives inner joy and peace of mind."[4]

You may wonder, then, what criteria should be used to determine if you need spiritual improvement in your pursuit of potential, work, or relationships. Simply stated, there is a spiritual dysfunction in any of these areas when the interaction between you and the person in any of those relationships is not mutually satisfying. The concept of mutual must be emphasized. In other words, it's not just your assessment that counts in deciding if you're spiritual.

You may feel that your work and your relationships are fully acceptable to you. But if your employer or relational persons are not satisfied, there is a spiritual dysfunction. On the other hand, your employer and your relational persons may herald your praises in those roles. But if you are superficially going through the motions (roles) while internally unhappy, there is, again, a spiritual dysfunction.

For a reason unknown to me, there is an extremely conspicuous absence in addressing the daily work and relationship aspects of life among the many martial artists who routinely refer to the "spiritual." Too often, spirituality is thought to be limited to some sort of esoteric, "enlightenment," or *"satori"* experience wherein one would suddenly perform effortlessly and "without thought." Or in terms of the everyday world, the spirituality I often see portrayed is some sort of passionless, passive attitude toward undesirable activities. As kung-fu author Mark Salzman described his father in *Lost in Place*,[5] there seems to be a tendency to not so much experience, but endure life.

Since the fundamental methods of Zen are passive,[6] I anticipate there is probably apprehension about an introspection that addresses work and relationships. For one, it is very possible that you have not been previously challenged in this manner which could, quite naturally, create a tendency to withdraw. Secondly, if you're a committed martial artist that has "progressed" on a steady diet of technical and traditional training, you may question the relevance of the Total Quality approach.

Just as other sport's professional athletes have demonstrated, the martial arts also offer examples of what can happen when spiritual needs are ignored in favor of purely physical concerns. One California-based martial artist was sentenced to prison for inappropriate sexual behavior with under age students. A famous referee served time in prison for drugs. One of our most visible action stars had to submit himself for drug rehabilitation.[7] Three of the top martial movie stars in 1996 have been divorced, two of them three times apiece. You may initially think, "divorced? What's the big deal?"

Maybe none. But if the "spirituality" of the martial arts has any meaningful relevance to our everyday lives, then it must affect how we interact in our relationships: with our intimate partners and families, other martial artists, children, employers, coworkers—basically everyone in our personal universe. Spirituality isn't just measured by the ability to endure strenuous physical training.

In Total Quality Martial Arts, the premise is that any unrealized potential you have as an athlete may well be the result of spiritual disharmony, not simply a lack of training. This spiritual disharmony may express itself in alcohol, in sex, in absenteeism from work or in the end of a marriage. In purely athletic terms, it may show up in the athlete who, although highly talented, is always injured or experiencing some misfortune that precludes the full realization of potential. Sometimes, these results of disharmony may be quite delayed. But in the course of life and performance, they always appear.

As stated previously, most athletes think that everything will be great once they achieve their athletic goal. But world class athletes like Magic Johnson, Mickey Mantle, O.J. Simpson, and Tommy Morrison demonstrate that "being okay" requires more than physical performance, recognition, and achievement.

Dr. Michael Maliszewski[8] has noted that a problem exists in the martial arts among those who are absorbed in the physical dimensions to the exclusion of the spiritual components. Many may become proficient in technical skills while remaining in a stagnated psychological state of immaturity, particularly among those who began the martial arts because of a traumatic experience or feelings of inadequacy and impotence.

Stephen Covey[9] has pointed out that private victories precede public victories. We all want that dramatic win in competition or realization of personal potential. But the roots of competitive victory are formed in the quiet caverns of the soul. In addition to the purely physical and scientific aspects, these roots are grounded in the spiritual discipline and harmony among one's understanding and pursuit of potential as well as work and relationships.

To fully adopt our Total Quality approach, we'll review potential in

Chapter Five, vocation in Chapter Six, and relationships in Chapter Seven. These three important spiritual considerations will enable us to live in accordance with that unseen order of things.

CHAPTER FIVE

ASSESSING POTENTIAL

> *"The only sin is mediocrity."*
> —Martha Graham

We are not mediocre martial athletes if we never visit, let alone win, a national tournament. We're mediocre if we have national ability and don't develop it. If we don't have the ability to be a national champion but "aspire" to be one, we're not mediocre but delusional. The difference, as I've alluded to previously, is a function of our potential.

Since true spirituality means to live in accordance with an unseen order of things, we must understand our potential as an expression of that "unseen" order. Our inherited potential is an "unseen" order of mental temperament and certain physical characteristics (such as muscle fiber type) that predisposes us toward certain physical activities and levels of competition. In turn, this affects not only how we view the martial arts, but how we look at our daily vocations and, in turn, tremendously affects our relationships.

To talk about our individual potential requires a willingness to be objective. This means to examine our potential based on quantifiable standards and not a mental image. We can't say we'll be the next great American kickboxer because we like or identify with a certain movie star or known competitor. Great kickboxers demonstrate certain physical characteristics that create standards for us to measure ourselves against. That's what I mean by objective.

Some of you may be thinking you have no real interest in whether or not you have elite competitor potential. You may be saying you just like to train and stay in shape. But I suggest that you should look at the subject of potential now, rather than later, because in one way or another, athletes usually come to a point in their lives where they want to push the limits.

We are in the information age and are constantly bombarded by the stories of athletes who are trying to adjust the limits of human performance. Too often, we have a mental image that says "I can do that too" without having any scientific or objective reference for that aspiration. In this chapter, I can help save you some frustration or help you en route to a vision that is grounded in reality.

My own personal history offers a revealing example. When I began competitive bicycle racing, I perceived a type of curse that I did not understand at the time. Riding with many racers, even some "notable" ones, bored me. I was clearly better. But when I attempted to compete with "distinguished" racers from a more regional basis, I was just off the back. I often wondered what it would take to either stretch myself to catch the distinguished or allow myself to "slide down" the ladder of expectations.

At that time, I frequently identified with the character of Salieri in the play Amadeus. Salieri lamented his perceived curse from God by wondering why he was given such a sensitivity to music without a corresponding ability to play it in such a manner as Wolfgang Amadeus Mozart. In my heart, I saw myself as the Salieri of bicycle racing.

For almost a decade I cursed this misfortune. I said to myself that I would prefer to clearly have the ability of either the average or the distinguished group. Finding myself in the middle was an uncomfortable and lonely experience.

What I did not understand in those early years was the significance of the VO_2 max (maximum ability to consume oxygen) as a predictor of endurance type competition. If I had known about and compared myself against this objective standard early on, I could have gotten on about the business of spiritual growth and racing within my potential much sooner. But prior to an exposure to science-based standards, I based my aspirations on what I saw in my mind. That gave me numerous years of frustration until I finally understood the role of VO_2 max as a predictor of performance in cycling.

I am not alone, however. On numerous occasions I have heard athletes state they are "going pro" based on their vicarious experience of an event totally unrelated to themselves—such as viewing a movie or an athletic event. In the case of athletes who have true potential, stimulation for elite competition through movies or events is appropriate. But not if the potential isn't there.

To become spiritually mature and perform in accordance with our inherent ability, a basic understanding must be accepted: elite athletes are genetically gifted. The term "elite," in this context, does not have a negative connotation such as the culturally elite. In this athletic sense it simply means "unique." If these genetic gifts were germane to everyone, there would be no elite, or unique athletes.

As the next step in Total Quality Martial Arts, we'll look at some objective standards you can use to determine your potential. Once again, it's data gathering research and an objective process with standards that distinguishes the Total Quality approach from more generalized thinking. Generalized thinking is a bit dreamlike—picturing what we might be. The Total Quality approach uses science as a reality check. Once we've stopped and absorbed the facts at that station, we then pursue our true, individualized potential.

Determining Martial Art Potential— Temperament

Have you ever wondered what top-notch boxers like Mike Tyson, Joe Frazier, Larry Holmes, and Thomas Hearns have in common? Besides a desire to destroy their opponents, these fighters and similar superstars also have the same mindset, or "temperament." This is a scientifically verified temperament that is genetically determined.

> Fighters and similar superstars also have the same mindset, or temperament.

The renowned psychologist Dr. Carl Jung founded the modern theory of psychological "type." In his theory, "type" is a summary of eight personality preferences that broadly describe all people. These preferences characterize whether you are extroverted or introverted, sensing or intuitive, a thinker or feeler, and judging or perceiving.

Jung's theory concerning type was refined and validated in over 40 years of scientific research by other psychologists who developed what is known as the Myers-Briggs Type Indicator (MBTI). While type describes very specific preferences, temperament describes four broader categories that all the types fit into. Numerous successful sports coaches and business corporations use the type indicator to predict an individual's potential success. The instrument has demonstrated an 87% reliability index in accurately assessing type.

One expert in this use of psychological type has determined the common temperament among the most recognized names in the combat sports of boxing and wrestling. In his book, *Your Best Sport*,[1] sports scientist and typologist Jon Niednagel shows how Tyson, Sugar Ray Leonard, Ken Norton, and a host of other heavy hitters are all of the "SP" temperament. Although the martial arts are not included in his review of combat sports, the prevalence of this temperament among boxers and wrestlers, in particular, suggests that Niednagel's research generally applies to any individual combat sport. Among the martial athletes I've "typed," the ones successful in competition have, without exception, been of the "SP" temperament.

This "SP" temperament designation describes people whose preferences include sensing and perceiving. A sensor is a person who prefers to see the world through their five senses whereas the opposite preference, intuition, prefers the world of imagination. As a perceiver, a person prefers a flexible lifestyle while the opposite preference, judging, prefers a structured lifestyle.

To get an initial grasp on what your temperament might be, try answering these simple questions: Do you prefer facts and practical matters or ideas and creativity? Do you prefer keeping your options open or making quick decisions? If you selected the first statement in both sentences, there's a chance you could be an "SP" like Roberto Duran or Riddick Bowe.

The other three temperaments include the NF, NT, and SJ. While Niednagel documents hundreds of successful athletes among those three tem-

1998 Pan-Am Gold Medalist Mark Long is an "SP"—the mental temperament of choice among competitive martial athletes

peraments, successful combat athletes in boxing and wrestling are all "SP." While answering questions like "do you prefer facts or ideas" may not initially seem related to success in combat sports, psychological type shows the physical implications of the eight preferences. This is because an analysis of the temperaments demonstrates which combination of preferences have the greatest gross motor skills, dexterity, and body rhythm. Overall, the "SP" temperament contains the physical and mental motor skills necessary to compete at the elite levels of combat sports.

I am presenting this mental temperament standard first among the standards of potential because in my experience with type theory and sports, this is probably even more crucial than the physical characteristics we'll review shortly. Have you ever see someone trying to practice the martial arts that just didn't seem to "get it?" I mean they tried and tried but no matter what the movements seem a little too stiff, a little too awkward? Chances are you're observing someone who is not an "SP;" someone without the inherent motor skills it takes to move fluidly and gracefully.

Please understand that this doesn't mean only "SP" temperaments are qualified for the martial arts. All four temperaments can be found practicing. What I'm talking about here is potential, both relative to yourself and against competition. While you may be a non-"SP" and enjoying the arts quite well, temperament type research demonstrates that your access to the elite levels of competition in combat sports is severely inhibited.

My recommendation is that you complete the MBTI instrument to determine your precise type and temperament. This is not only useful for determining your potential in combat sports, but may also help you in selecting the most appropriate career and with interpersonal relationships. The indicator is used by numerous counselors for these very purposes. Since function follows form, it is important to remember that people will express themselves according to their inherited temperaments. Besides the athletic considerations, a majority of the people you regularly interact with will make you grind your teeth if you don't understand the basis of their temperament.

By using the MBTI indicator and its characteristics, Jon Neidnagel has consulted and successfully "typed" hundreds of athletes in the NBA and NFL. This includes a recommendation to former Dallas Cowboy's coach Tom Landry to select a then unknown UCLA quarterback named Troy Aikman. Use of the MBTI in predicating success can help you as well.

Furthermore, the research in *Your Best Sport* demonstrates that an "STP" will have fine motor skills, such as precise hand movements, while the "SFP" will have better gross motor skills, or overall body coordination. Along with Troy Aikman, Niednagel shows how this is seen among star athletes such as Magic Johnson, Michael Jordan, Dennis Rodman, and Carl Lewis. In turn, you can use this instrument to help assess your own, and other martial artists', potential just as it has been used to successfully predict the potential of many sport's athletes.

Neidnagel's book has an abbreviated "test" or you can order copies of the MBTI instrument by using the information provided in the Appendix. Based on my research and observation, I emphasize that this temperament consideration is probably the most important factor of all in determining potential.

Determining Martial Art Potential—
Elite Physical Comparisons

A Canadian research study published in 1995 confirms that top kickboxers are among the best of all athletes, not just kickboxers, and possess certain characteristics that distinguish them from amateur athletes.[2] As a landmark study of quantifying the physical characteristics of certain martial artists, this information can be used to make certain conclusions about other systems and not just kickboxing. After reviewing the study, we'll examine some of those general conclusions.

Randy Zabukovec and Peter M. Tiidus of Wilfrid Laurier University in Ontario published their findings in the *Journal of Strength and Conditioning Research* and demonstrated that the kickboxing superstars we have admired are indeed elite athletes. Let's review the standards they set and see if you have what it takes. The research was conducted with elite male kickboxers and reveals exceptional fitness in four critical performance areas.

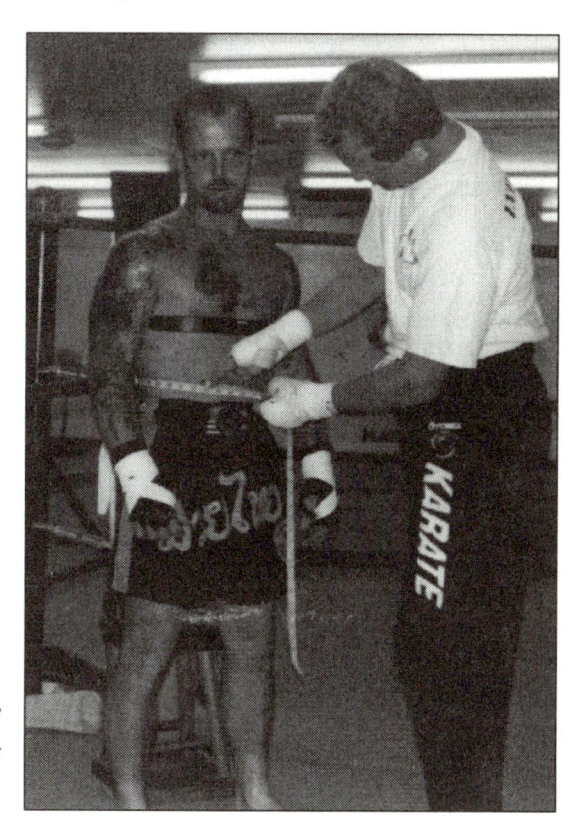

K.I.C.K. welterweight champion Doug Freeman has his bodyfat measured.

1. **High aerobic capacity.** Aerobic activity, from the laymen's perspective, is generally understood as the ability to perform extended exercise at moderate intensity (usually 65–85% of maximum heart rate for more than 20 minutes). In controlled laboratory measurements, elite kickboxers had recorded values of aerobic capacity that are comparable to a person who runs a 4:45 mile, or a 34 minute 10k foot race. This doesn't mean these kickboxers could necessarily run at those speeds (without specific training), but their aerobic values are the same as those who do.

2. **High anaerobic capacity.** Anaerobic activity is characterized by short, intense efforts performed in the absence of molecular oxygen, usually up to six seconds in length. This study revealed that elite kickboxers have higher values than elite American wrestlers. In fact, the recorded values place elite kickboxers above the 95th percentile of the entire male population!

3. **Knee extension peak torque.** One laboratory test measured the magnitude of force generated by the knee at various joint angles to demonstrate peak torque. The test subject's results were similar to elite Alpine skiers and only slightly lower than elite sprinters and jumpers.

4. **Low body fat.** At an mean weight of 160 pounds, the average body fat percentage among these kickboxers was 8.1%— which is similar to that found in elite male endurance athletes. Furthermore, this 8.1% is substantially lower than the 12 to 15% average among elite boxers.

So what about you? Do you think you might have these four characteristics. On the one hand, you could research that study and go to your local university sport center and be tested to determine if you meet the same standards expressed in those findings. But short of that, I'll provide you with two tests you can administer to yourself at no cost to make an initial determination of how you compare. This includes the VO_2 max and an assessment of your muscle fiber type.

VO2 Max Test

To determine your aerobic capacity, this assessment merely requires you to run on a quarter mile track. This method is called the "twelve minute test."[3] To assess the VO2 max, run as many laps as possible within 12 minutes. Based on the number of laps run, you will have the corresponding (approximate) values:

Laps	Distance	VO_2
4	1.0	25
5	1.25	33
6	1.5	42
7	1.75	51
8	2.0	60

The advantage to this method is that it is accessible to everyone and only costs 12 minutes of time. The disadvantage is that it is not as precise as laboratory assessments and will take some number crunching to determine values that do not represent complete laps.

To have characteristics similar to elite kickboxers, you would need to run slightly over eight laps in your test because their average VO_2 max is approximately 62. But let's say you only complete six laps. Can you simply run more and reach these elite levels? In his book *The Lore of Running*,[4] Timothy Noakes demonstrates that the VO_2 max of any individual, whether elite or average, can only be increased by five to 15% with even the most intense training. This is a significant consideration in determining elite potential.

For instance, if you have a VO_2 Max of 42 (the average among healthy males), this means that with intense training and good fortune, the most you could hope to raise your VO_2 max would be to 48, assuming a 15% increase. This leaves you a long distance from the elite kickboxers with an average of 62. This explains why some competitors, despite rigorous training, still "suck wind" against more genetically gifted athletes. A genetically gifted athlete may have a starting VO_2 max of 60. Then, with even a 5% increase, although not as significant as a 15% increase, the VO_2 max is 63—the elite level of professional kickboxers. As the old saying goes, you have to choose your parents well.

This research, then, clearly demonstrates implications for every aspiring martial athlete as well as athletes of any sport with a cardiovascular base. If I would have been aware of these VO_2 max considerations when I began bicycle racing, I would have definitely approached my training in an entirely different manner. In slight contrast to kickboxing, the average (bottom) value among elite cyclists is 67 while my very highest value, at age 21, was only 62 (now in my third decade of life I'm in the mid-50s—it does decrease with age). Going back to the introduction of this chapter, these values explain why I felt juxtaposed between the "notable" and "distinguished" groups of racers. You see, had I been armed with this knowledge at an earlier age, I could have accepted my fate and made better, corresponding decisions about spiritual and athletic matters.

In determining your potential, if you have any aspirations beyond amateur competition, it is absolutely imperative that you conduct a VO_2 Max test to determine the reasonableness of your pursuit. If you don't, you too may carry unnecessary attitudes and unreal expectations. By using the 12 minute test provided in this section, you have an empirically developed method of assessment that enables you to take the first step of objective comparison in determining who you are—your "unseen" order of things.

Muscle Fiber Type

To test your potential for anaerobic capacity, we'll use the same self-assessment test from Chapter Three. Remember in Chapter One we reviewed the differences in muscle fibers—how Type I is used for lower intensity (aerobic) efforts and Type II is used for higher intensity (anaerobic) efforts. Like the 12 minute test, you can determine your approximate muscle-fiber type outside of the laboratory at absolutely no cost other than a visit to the local gym. Just use the following assessment as you did in Chapter Three. Here are the instructions again.

Using the quadriceps extension exercise, determine what your one repetition maximum is. This may take a few tries and, if a few attempts are necessary, wait five minutes between attempts to ensure you have rested muscles for these maximal efforts.

Once you have determined your one repetition maximum, take 70% of that amount and try to perform as many repetitions as possible. Based on the amount of repetitions you perform with that 70% of maximum, your fiber type can be approximated to be the following:

1–9	Fast twitch	Type IIB (fewer repetitions = greater amount of Type II fibers)
10–11	Intermediate	Type IIA
12 +	Slow twitch	Type I (more fatigue resistant = able to do more repetitions)

The difference in fiber types directly impacts the types of sport activities you are attracted to and your potential within those activities. Elite runners, for instance, have a predominance of Type I, slow-twitch oxidative fibers. This allows them to sustain work over a long duration due to the oxidative nature of their fiber type.

Then there are those with Type IIB fibers whose output is explosive but also more vulnerable to fatigue due to the lack of oxidative fibers. These are the track and field type of athletes: sprinters, javelin throwers, and other types of "power" athletes. You won't see these types of athletes lining up at the next 10k running race.

And finally there are those with the intermediate, or Type IIA fibers. These are elite kickboxer types. They have enough power in their legs to deliver devastating kicks by virtue of the type II fibers. They have enough endurance to keep kicking round after round due to the presence of some oxidative fibers. With too many Type I fibers, there wouldn't be enough power. With too many Type IIB fibers, not enough endurance. Elite martial athletes whose competition requires sustained duration, even with intermittent breaks, possess intermediate fibers. So, how do you aply this knowledge?

Let's assume that you are a dedicated martial artist who trains eight to 10 hours a week and are therefore in good physical fitness. One afternoon you see a kickboxing match and the event appeals to you; suddenly, you want to "go pro." If you want to objectively decide whether you have a chance, take some time to determine who you are as an athlete before you invest the time and effort into emulating what you have seen on the screen. Run the track, perform the muscle fiber assessment. These are two assessments you can perform at no cost and they will provide you with an indication of your inherited potential.

Concerning the third and forth standards set by the elite kickboxers in that research study (knee torque extension and body fat), my research indicates that these characteristics are trainable and not restricted to a "genetic inheritance." Thus, I'm not providing a means of self-assessment for these two standards, although you can easily have these determined if you are interested in comparing yourself to all aspects of the study.

It should be noted that this muscle fiber test can also be performed for the upper body, such as the biceps curl and bench press. Like the quadriceps test, the results will tell you whether you have fast, slow, or intermediate twitch type muscles in the upper body. Incidentally, assessing your biceps and pectoralis muscle groups will tell you wether you have any bodybuilding potential. The ultimate potential for increased muscle mass (termed "hypertrophy") is determined by the amount of fast twitch muscle fibers you possess. If you have a low amount (your muscles are more oxidative in nature) you won't get the phenomenal gains seen in elite bodybuilders—no matter how hard you work. This is yet another example of why it's important to use objective standards when deciding on a sport goal and training program.

You see, muscle fiber composition is a relatively fixed inheritance you received at birth. There may be a small conversion of Type IIB fibers into Type IIA, but the only significant changes from training really concern the enzyme systems associated with those fibers, not the fibers themselves. In other words, although you may have a low amount of Type IIB fibers, you can train and maximize those you have by developing the phosphagen stores (referenced in Chapter One). But like the VO_2 max example, your maximum development of a (comparatively) lower percentage of Type IIB fibers may still be less than a under-trained but more genetically athlete with a higher amount of inherited Type IIB fibers.

Refining Potential

Let us now assume that you've tested as an "SP" mental temperament and therefore have one of the essential building blocks of martial athlete excellence. Moreover, let's assume that you've performed the two self-assessments and determined you have a high VO2 max and intermediate muscle fibers. Based on these assumptions, you're ready to begin training for elite competition. How should you train if your aspirations are beyond point fighting and you want characteristics like those elite kickboxers?

1. Increase your aerobic capacity. Although running is convenient for time management, cycling or swimming is perhaps the best alternative. Due to the extensive use of the knees in normal martial art training, a non-impact aerobic activity is more beneficial. Low intensity cycling will also facilitate removal of lactic acid (that byproduct of high intensity training discussed in Chapter One).

Three sessions of 20 minute duration per week creates an aerobic base ready for top performance—it's not an everyday necessity. To be aerobic, the intensity should be between 65 to 85% of your maximum heart rate (see Chapter Two for calculating maximum heart rate).

2. Increase your anaerobic capacity. This will probably require a coach, or at a minimum, a strong peer network to ensure truly high intensity efforts. To increase anaerobic capacity, perform short (one to six second) maximum intensity efforts with (varying) 20 to 60 second recovery periods between sets. In sparring, don't settle into the habit of trading single strike movements with your partner. Attack in a flurry!

3. Increase your knee extension peak torque. The best overall method for this is systematic resistance (weight) training that incorporates squats, lunges, and quadriceps extensions. However, by cycling or swimming you can work on both aerobic capacity and knee torque at the same time.

4. Decrease your percentage of body fat. To achieve the kind of percentages measured in those elite kickboxers, you must emphasize sound nutrition in addition to high-quality training. Without detailing all the facts on balanced

diets and food groups, let me give you the easiest-to-remember piece of encouragement that will change your body fat percentage: don't eat anything over 30% in fat content.

When looking at a manufacturer's label, multiply the fat gram content by nine and determine the percentage of fat compared to the overall amount of calories in the item. For example, if a suggested serving size has 200 total calories and there are nine grams of fat, that means 81 of the 200 total calories are fat (or 40.5%). Don't overlook this facet of nutrition planning.

General Conclusions

Okay, you may say, "that's all very interesting stuff about elite kickboxers but I don't kickbox." Nevertheless, these research findings, when combined with a basic understanding of the human body (as identified in Chapter One) provides you with the ability to make certain comparisons about your preferred martial art.

For example, let's say your art or system is street defense. You're not looking to last several rounds in the ring—you want maximum "one punch" (or kick) power. Do you have what it takes? If you tested as having a high proportion of Type IIB muscle fibers, you very likely do. Training in more endurance type systems of martial arts will not be as beneficial for you. On the other hand, let's say you practice judo. What are the energy demands? Short bursts of high energy interspersed with periods of medium intensity. The best fibers? Type IIA with training of both the phosphagen and glycolytic energy systems.

You see, understanding the basic systems and fibers allows you to interpret what you need in training. The Canadian research study reinforces this. And perhaps even more importantly, it allows you to determine what your potential is in a certain martial art before you even begin. If you have Type IIB fibers, you will be best suited in point-style fighting where the oxidative system plays a minor role. If Type IIA, kickboxing would be appropriate. And frankly, if your muscle fiber results demonstrate Type I, you are probably better suited with a sport other than the martial arts, such as distance running, cycling, or swimming.

In the final analysis, potential is not just a matter of willpower or commitment. As I stated in the beginning of this book, all athletes are not created equal. Nor do all athletes have the same opportunity for elite competition without the right building blocks. In elite martial arts, potential is expressed in the "SP" temperament, Type IIA muscle fiber type, and a high VO_2 max.

> **Potential is not just a matter of willpower or commitment.**

Understanding this is a crucial step in your spiritual growth. Without these elements, training can be fruitless if the goal is simply outside your capacity. Be spiritual, then, and set your martial art goals in accordance with the unseen order of your genetic inheritance.

CHAPTER SIX

VOCATION

"Either what we do every-day is important or nothing is."
—GEORGE SHEEHAN

Once you have objectively ascertained your potential, the next spiritual step is to examine your vocation. Understanding our potential comes first, because afterwards we naturally serve others by becoming who we are.[1] In other words, you won't have to do "special" things or champion certain causes to be spiritual. Some have suggested that the measure of spirituality is seen in a quietness, settledness, or balanced energy.[2] In Total Quality Martial Arts, true spirituality is practicing your art and pursuing a viable potential while naturally serving others in your work and relationships.

If your potential is not as a professional martial artist, you'll be among the millions of practitioners worldwide who also work in a capacity outside the martial arts. I know of almost no one who is committed to the martial arts that hasn't contemplated what it would be like to teach as a full-time profession. But as the high incidence of "fly-by-night" schools demonstrate, it's a tough market as an instructor and there will always be tremendously more "bivocational" martial artists than those who actually perform the arts as a profession.

Vocation is a Spiritual Matter

Among the martial art authors who address the topic of spirituality, there is a conspicuous absence concerning vocation among those who don't perform the arts as a living. But to become spiritual, this is obviously a very crucial aspect. As a practical matter, if you're not making a living as a martial artist, such as competing or teaching, then you're spending at least one-third of your life in your vocation. If you subtract sleep, then you're spending one-half or more of your conscious time in something that probably doesn't relate to the martial arts. Clearly, then, vocation is a matter of spiritual concern.

> Do you regard what you do everyday as important and fulfilling? The answer reflects your spirituality.

There are many people who only look at life, and work in particular, as something to tolerate in between martial arts or similar athletic activities. In turn, your attitude and practice of work has a reciprocal relationship to your martial art—one affects the other. Do you regard what you do everyday as worthy of investing your energy and attention? To be spiritual means to be fully engaged in the moment—even if that moment is a temporary position or school experience. In turn, developing spiritual habits in life situations outside the martial arts will help you become a Total Quality martial artist.

Placement and Attitude

If you are not satisfied in your non-martial arts employment situation, it could be due to one of two reasons. One is that you may be in the wrong vocation. The other is that you might have an unspiritual attitude toward that vocation. And what's more, if you are in the wrong vocation, then so is another person! For if you are in the wrong position, then someone who belongs in that position is unsatisfied in a misplaced position and should be there! So there's that "unseen" order of things again.

I often hear athletes complain that they could be achieving a much higher level of performance, perhaps even be a professional, if not for work. The Total Quality Martial Arts approach to athletics provides some objective standards to help you decide whether that is a viable alternative. As I demonstrated in Chapter Five, an aspiration to be a professional kickboxer, for instance, is available to those who possess certain physical characteristics; so is elite endurance running, bodybuilding, and the like.

After reading those performance predictor indicators in Chapter Five, you should know precisely whether you have a role in elite athletics or not. If you have an "SP" temperament, certain muscle fibers and level of VO_2 max, then it is entirely reasonable for you to collect all the information necessary to train and pursue elite levels of competition. In effect, you have a choice. With an elite genetic endowment, you can pursue a corresponding athletic vocation. Or, if another vocation in life seems to compel you, you can forgo your genetic talent in favor of what you individually deem as a more meaningful career.

If you do not have an elite genetic endowment, then you must take the step in self-honesty that concedes to an amateur athletic career. Or perhaps you can be a "bivocational" martial artist wherein you may not be making a living from the arts but serve in a capacity that supports them. We'll examine some of the alternatives at the end of this chapter. The bottom line is that if you're not competing or teaching for a living, a suitable vocation will be necessary to support your martial art interests as well as your other fundamental responsibilities such as a home and family.

Work Attitude

It is that non-professional martial art vocational reality that we address here as an important spiritual consideration. Even among the martial athletes who have conceded to an amateur capacity, I have still observed a tendency to resist or resent work (that "tolerating" life between training sessions). If it is clear that someone will not derive their living as a professional martial artist, why then would they have this attitude toward their ability for self or family support?

One reason may be due to a misunderstood application of Zen among those practicing a Japanese system of spiritual practice. While healthy and unhealthy habits undoubtedly exist among toher national styles such as Southeast Asian and India, my thoughts here will focus on the Japanese style of Zen in which I've grown. As I mentioned in the overview to this section, there are those who see spirituality through a perspective of passiveness, or indifference to the daily world. This is an outgrowth of the mistaken desire "to enter a life which is completely aimless,"[3] or that state of "no-mind." But as Jack Hobain observes, why subscribe to something that negates the self?[4] If, as some argue, Zen is about being wholly in the instant[5] (or moment), then won't work be an activity that deserves your full enthusiasm and energies?

> **If Zen is about being wholly in the moment, won't work be an activity that deserves your full enthusiasm and energies?**

Most adult martial artists must integrate professional vocations with dojo life.

Instead, what we often find within ourselves is a desire to be anywhere but in the moment. It's sort of like what basketball great Charles Barkley describes concerning his NBA peers: "This league is full of rappers and wanna-be movie stars. Everybody wants to do everything else except play the game."[6] This is because "the moment" has pain and we like to mentally create an effortless existence. Our challenge, then, is to experience a sense of energy and exuberance in the ordinary things of life.

Aside from a misunderstanding of Zen, two other possible causes include being in the wrong employment position or possessing a wrong attitude toward the employment. It could also be the simple tension of trying to meet the tough commitments of work and martial arts practice; the assumption being that the martial arts are the favored activity. Needless to say, these are two tough commitments to integrate. The martial arts are not like the fitness-only enthusiast who merely runs at lunch or the person who plays handball for an hour in the afternoon. Martial arts is a time-intensive activity that requires the skillful art of integration, such as "training in the margins" that I introduced in Chapter Two.

Vocational Assessment

If you believe that you are in the wrong vocation, there are a wealth of resources that can help you identify where you should be. One of the best beginning points is, once again, the same Myers-Briggs Type Indicator that was discussed in Chapter Four as a predictor of athletic achievement. Just as the types and temperaments indicate which athletic capacity is probably best for you, there are literally hundreds of examples that indicate what vocations your particular type might seek and which should be avoided. It can also help identify which types of partners you will be most compatible with in a relationship.

The Myers-Briggs assessment is used increasingly among college students as well as among those suffering from mid-life ambiguity about their employment. And yet, it is only one of many assessments that a person can use to find a vocational "best fit." Amateur athletes, as well as any person who is not satisfied in their employment, should seek out an empirical tool like this to help define their unique design in life.

Dissatisfaction

Sometimes an unhappy person will seek this assessment to find their "true vocation" and find that it indicates they are already within their very preferences. If you are functioning within your preferences and are still unsatisfied, then we must examine the second possible reason for the "bivocational strain": the spiritual attitude toward work.

Marsha Sinetar[7] identifies a cause of bad attitudes among those who resent work. Those who demonstrate a bad attitude toward their work may do so because they are unloving. Sinetar has discovered that when we are unloving toward ourselves or toward others, we carry a hostile attitude toward the responsibility of work and express those hostile feelings in our daily duties. Other factors may induce hostility, such as an unjust work environment, but we should first rigorously examine ourselves before we assign responsibility to external circumstances.

Just as there is no infusion to raise physical performance levels automatically (it takes training!), people do not automatically become loving toward themselves or others in a mere moment if it's more loving that is needed. If you know you are destined to be an amateur and also know that you are essentially within your best-fit vocation and yet still experience dissatisfaction in your employment, this unlovingness may well be the cause. Unfortunately, a state such as this is created over a long period of time and will therefore take considerable effort to discern and dispel its origin.

Committment to Life

This tendency to be unloving, to have a low commitment to our daily lives, is a fundamental concern addressed in the Total Quality Martial Arts approach. Unfortunately, too often we read about some sort of misguided use of *"satori,"* "enlightenment," or Zen-like approach to work and spiritually. These perspectives are often misrepresented and used to encourage a sort of "non-attachment" to work where you essentially withdraw from unpleasant circumstances and act like those circumstances don't bother you. In this misguided approach, "enlightenment" is some state to achieve; a point where we're separate and unconnected to the external world. But that approach won't serve your deep human needs.

As Charlotte Joko Beck demonstrates in her excellent books *Nothing Special: Living Zen*[8] and *Everyday Zen*,[9] when we try to protect ourselves by withdrawing or being unattached, we clog up our lives and the life flow stagnates. In that perspective, life and work are merely something to tolerate between martial arts activities.

But to be spiritual, there can no division in your life by regarding practice as spiritual and work as mundane. If we practice that type of division, will find ourselves daydreaming, or wishing to be somewhere else. True Zen, as Charlotte Beck points out, is returning to the moment—no daydreaming or acting as if it doesn't matter. You will not find "truth" in something you use to avoid it.

> You will not find "truth" in something you use to avoid it.

Your truth is right here: now. Don't forget that the opposite of present is not past or future, but absent. Moreover, your spiritual perspective will not only affect how you train, but also what you do off the mat as a daily service and in your core relationships (which will be discussed in the next chapter).

Total Quality Means Work, Too

We must address the total sum of your life: training, work, and relationships. Is any so-called spirituality really worth its weight if it's only restricted to one aspect of your life? The ability to endure an hour of super high intensity training is, to a degree, a spiritual matter. But so is the need to effectively deal with supervisors, fellow employees, and the product or service you help deliver to customers. It is therefore critical for you to bring the aspect of employment into harmony in your life. If you don't, you may sacrifice a meaningful career in order to work in a less strenuous job that allows you to train during the day. I have known and read of many would-be professionals who suffer this frustration. But if your genetic performance indicator does not substantiate the practicality of this sacrifice, then you are wasting an unknown amount of productive years of service that would be beneficial for you as well as society.

Be gracious to yourself. If you are not destined to be a national champion, then use your talents to develop a fully satisfying vocation that features martial arts as an avocation. Treat your work as a gift and as an important spiritual matter where you demonstrate a good attitude and workmanship. If you are alive, healthy, and capable of working, then you have been gifted! Give yourself "permission" to be fully human and, in proportion, pursue your love of the martial arts.

Vocational Alternatives

Let's assume that you're a spiritually mature person and you've read and conceded to an amateur disposition as a martial artist and further understand the need for a proper perspective and attitude toward employment. Yet, you may still feel a gnawing, a compulsion, really, toward the martial arts. Perhaps you sense within yourself that if you are not destined to a career where you physically perform martial arts, you would like to pursue a vocation that is martial art related.

> "Any talent you're born with rises up as a need."
> —Marsha Sinetar

If this is true of you, there are many vocations that will enable you to be close to the martial arts. But first, it is important to understand some fundamental things that are characteristic of any career change or career pursuit related to the martial arts. In other words, don't give up your day job—yet.

Just because individuals are genetically gifted to be athletes, they don't automatically become successful (paid) performers. It takes long term development, which includes the skills of planning and training. And so, if you desire to pursue a martial arts-related vocation, it will require an intelligent, comprehensive approach.

Vocational Planning

Sometimes we fail to have the vocation we want in life because we do not adequately plan for it. Many people wish for a martial arts-related vocation. But if you merely wish for it and then carry on about your life without doing anything about it, you will probably not seize an opportunity to fulfill your wish if given the chance. Remember, wishing is passive, choosing is active.

As an example, let's suppose you wish you could become a photographer. You'd like to capture the martial arts training, tournaments, and celebrity seminars with exceptional photography. You are convinced that this would satisfy you. But to become a photographer might mean an initial change in your financial situation, such as a salary decrease. It would also require a small investment to attend photography training and to purchase equipment. If you happen to make a larger salary in your current position or are without the training and equipment funds, you may not pursue this wish. Two years later, a professional photographer who has seen your improvisional skills offers you a position and states he will also pay your fees for photography training and equipment costs. Can you accept this position now? If you previously stayed in your employment because of a higher salary and spent your income accordingly, you still cannot take the lower paying position, even with free training and equipment.

Planning Means Choosing

Now, what if you choose to become a photographer? Go back two years in this story. When confronted with the decreased salary and photography training and equipment costs, you realized that you could not pursue that vocation at that particular time. But, in choosing to become a photographer, you decided to begin laying a foundation that would eventually allow you to make a transition.

So, instead of *wishing* you began *saving* a specified portion of your salary each month. More than saving, though, you began investing in mutual funds and now have a healthy economic reserve. In this scenario, when the professional photographer offers you the position, you can accept it! In choosing, you planned ahead.

Although accepting the position initially means less salary, you have created an economic resource that will prevent you from decreasing your standard of living. By using the "employment transition savings plan," you can proceed as a journeyman photographer and economically survive until you receive future salary increases or perhaps begin your own business. Then you can replenish the fund and perhaps make another transition in future years!

"Can't" May Mean "Won't"

What this story shows us is that we often fail to prepare ourselves for what we really want. To say that we "can't" pursue a particular vocation due to financial restraints often means that we won't do whatever is necessary to see our dream become a reality. In our lack of preparation, then, we experience fear at the point of opportunity. Whether you are someone who wants to become an elite athlete or someone who wants to pursue a martial arts-related vocation, you must realize that you may need to support your passion before it will support you.

You may need to support your passion before it will support you.

Marsha Sinetar states that "right livelihood" is a tough love, not an easy one. Because we vicariously experience or anticipate vocational pleasure based on what we see in mediums such as movies, we often envision our wished-for careers as effortless. Furthermore, we're often seeing the fruit of someone's vocation, not the root. In other words, we envy what they do but do not appreciate the price they paid to do it.

We must exercise the discipline to create or pursue our vocation carefully. As a function of increasing spiritual maturity, we can eventually become the elite or masters in a given field. Once we pay the price through training, planning, or savings, we are privileged to be paid. This takes time and is a measure of our true commitment to our vocational vision of ourselves.

An Analogy

Think of how parents financially support children until they have become mature enough to support themselves. Almost without exception, elite athletes or people desiring a martial arts-related vocation will also be required to support their passion until that skill is mature enough to support the person.

Again, you may have to support the development of the skill until it is able to support you.

How many eight-year-old children become a doctor at that age because they "wish" they could? None. A child's desire, talent, and skills are nurtured and perfected by years of training and education and then they are able to derive their living from their vocational love.

Be Realistic

Every vocation requires toil and effort. And every vocation requires "dogwork," those things that we don't want to do. Elite athletes spend a considerable amount of time traveling—something they may not care for but do because it is part of their career. The independent school owner must do accounting and bill collection although the true affection is interaction with the students. The message is simple: don't let the "dogwork" of your current vocation lead you to believe that you necessarily need a new one. Just as the oxygen debt mentioned in Chapter One can be misinterpreted as a call for aerobic training, "dogwork" can be misinterpreted as a need for a new vocation. Always remember the roots to the fruit you envy.

When we see a top competitor or seminar leader in action we think "Wow, I'd like to do that!" But that's like watching a football team or a movie for a couple of hours without seeing all the years of sweat and toil that lead to that experience. Regarding professional athletes, we say "a million bucks a year for a three hour game is good pay." But we don't consider the weight room, the playbook memorization, the physical toll, or the stress of having your next year of employment depend on a single game with an outcome that may be out of your control.

Marsha Sinetar states that spiritual discipline is not something dramatic but often something very ordinary or humble, e.g., the way that we approach the minutiae (dogwork). Every vocation has both the dramatic and the undramatic; the desirable and the undesirable. If you see something you'd like to do, check out the detriments as well as the advantages.

Superstars like Bill Wallace and Joe Lewis certainly enjoy a lot of prestige as seminar speakers but they pay a price for the demands of those vocations in

Superstar seminar leaders like Bill Wallace may spend almost every weekend away from home!

terms of their travel miles and weekends away from home. It is like that in vocations that support the martial arts as well. Check out Mike Dillard of Century uniforms and find out how he slept in his van in the early years of getting his uniform company off the ground. Remember that you can't enjoy the fruit without paying the price.

Vocational Alternatives

If you are still persuaded and still believe that there is a martial arts-related vocation that calls your name, then by all means begin to outline the steps that will lead to a successful transition. If your flesh and blood whisper to your unconscious and say "it's the martial arts" then exhaust all possibilities to properly align your life to support that call. Your role in that capacity may have benefits for yourself, for athletes, and for society that would not be realized if you don't pursue your love. While there are undoubtedly more than are outlined here, consider these martial art related vocations that may provide a suitable outlet for your interests.

1. Become an instructor. As opposed to the traditional school operator who may be trying it full time, you could pursue special outlets such as law enforcement training on a part-time basis.

2. Become a trainer. This could involve a four-year college degree (perhaps even a graduate degree), or could result from a program such as the Specialist in Martial Art Conditioning (SMAC) or Certified Strength and Conditioning Specialist (CSCS) study.

3. Become a physiologist or physical therapist, perhaps specializing in rehabilitation.

4. Become a dietician or nutritionist with an emphasis on anaerobic sports.

5. Become a masseuse specializing in joint flexibility.

6. Become a product marketing representative for a martial arts-related company.

7. Become an equipment engineer for training aids, uniforms, etc.

8. Become a journalist specializing in martial arts coverage.

9. Become an editor for a martial arts magazine.

10. Become an author or free-lance writer. This could mean writing articles or perhaps tournament summaries, or newsletters.

11. Become a photographer covering athletes in general and martial arts in particular.

12. Become a tournament (or festival) organizer, promoter, or sponsor.

13. Become a tournament referee.

14. Become a transportation organizer to help kids get to training and tournaments.

15. Become a software designer for computer programs that help martial artists analyze and improve their training and performance.

16. Become an administrative assistant or manager in an existing martial art

organization such as the National Association of Professional Martial Artists (NAPMA).

17. Own or manage a martial arts store.

18. Create and design special music for *katas* and training.

19. Create and design trophies and other forms of tangible recognition.

20. Become a martial arts historian.

21. Become an actor, producer, or similar type of involvement in martial arts cinema.

Conclusion: Don't be a Prisoner

You can unwittingly become a prisoner by thinking that all will be well at retirement—you won't have to "put up" with anything. But if you're waiting for retirement to solve your daily problems, you're like a sentenced convict merely biding your time. Don't be a victim. Aggressively address your vocational needs just as you practice your martial art.

First find out what vocation you're most suited to. Don't base this on what you've seen in the movies or even observed with close friends. Empirically determine your preferences with an instrument such as the Myers-Briggs assessment. Once in your position, seek to develop the best attitudes and product or service possible. Anything less is a spiritual compromise.

When it becomes clear that work is a spiritual matter that deserves our commitment and full attention, work flows much easier. But when we're unclear, dividing our lives into "spiritual" and "mundane" activities, our work is flawed, our relationships are flawed, and essentially any situation we participate in is flawed. Become spiritually minded about what you do on a daily basis. If it's not important, nothing is.

CHAPTER SEVEN

RELATIONSHIPS

> *"We cannot live for ourselves alone."*
> —HERMAN MELVILLE

The Spiritual Sequence in Total Quality Martial Arts

I have a reason why I have arranged the spiritual aspects discussed herein by potential, work, and now relationships. I addressed potential first because I presume that you are a martial artist and would like to know where you fit within that perspective first. I dealt with work second for two reasons. First, to help martial artists deal with the implications of a possibly non-professional pursuit of the arts. Second, because work, by hourly volume, represents so much of our lives, it pragmatically seems to appropriately appear second in the order of spiritual topics.

Next, relationships, and the opportunity for service, come out of our life tasks and work. And these naturally follow a determination of our potential and selected vocation. To be spiritual shouldn't be restricted to a certain designated part of our lives such as helping less fortunate people, although that is certainly important and can be a very spiritual activity. But how we treat our interpersonal relationships, as well as the relationships that occur in our tasks, is holistic spirituality—the Total Quality approach. This infers how we relate to the people at the post office, the grocery store, and in our work environment. Relationships come out of those tasks. "Hell may be other people," says George

Sheehan, "but the final enemy is within." If you can overcome yourself and authentically connect to others, you are on your way to achieving Total Quality Martial Arts.

Funakoshi on Families

The great karate master Gichin Funakoshi stated that we should show great concern for our families (and relationships). "The mind of the true *karateka* should be imbued with (family) concern before he turns his attention to his body and the refinement of his technique."[1] As human beings, we have a third dimension to address. The daily expression might not have the same volume as work, but the magnitude of relationships is perhaps most significant of all. Their magnitude is based on the fact that our core relationships deal with people we love; people who brought us into this world; people with whom we bring new persons in the world; and the children we birth and nurture.

The bond of blood is enormous. You may say, "True, but what does that

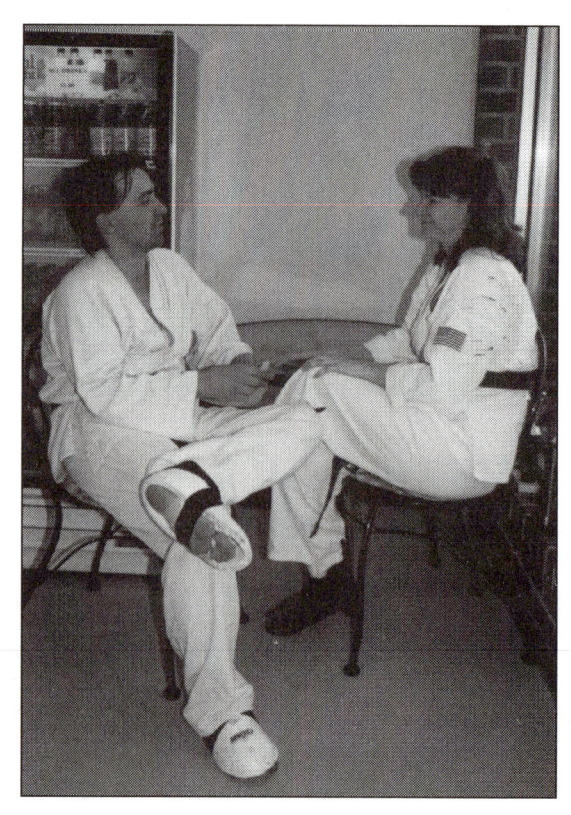

To be successful and spiritual means full attention to relationships off the mat as well as those in training.

have to do with my martial arts?" As a primary matter, do you really believe that you could give less honor or commitment to your relationships than your training and consider yourself spiritual? As a secondary matter, do you really believe that any disarray in your core relationships will not affect your martial art performance? Do you believe that you won't be distracted by unsettled issues with your parents, spouse, siblings, or children?

To be successful Total Quality martial artists, we must accept the challenge of managing different types of attention, both those concerning our art and those aspects that support it. *Aikidoist* Wendy Palmer describes two states of attention useful in this consideration.[2] The first type is "dropped attention," which describes a state where we have individual focus on ourselves and the subject matter at hand. This is the type of attention needed to achieve technical competency in the martial arts. It is practicing the techniques of our art in a repetitive manner with a narrow focus.

The second type is "open attention" and describes a state where we simultaneously maintain our dropped, or individual, attention while allowing other people or subject matters into our space. It doesn't mean we forgo the repetitions. To be open in this sense can mean we emphasize one thing (the art form) while addressing another (relationships). But if we don't see ourselves as connected in our relationships, they become a source of blame that may distract us during the practice of our art.

The Blame Game

Relationships, and the responsibility to maintain them, are what many martial athletes often cite as a detriment to their training and performance, just like the attitude toward work. Draw close to some of the athletes who are complaining about work interfering with their training and you will probably also hear reports about the relationships in their lives. "I couldn't get out to the dojo on Tuesday because my spouse/girlfriend/parents wanted me to spend time with them. Now I'll probably lose in the tournament this weekend."

Unfortunately, this may characterize you. Furthermore, it may be true. You may find, on occasion, that just as you are heading out the door for an important training session, someone who is a significant part of your life basically demands that you stop and give them some of the same time and energy that you are giving to your martial art pursuits. I call this the "arrest."

The Arrest

I have been "arrested" many times. In the early years of my now fifteen-year marriage, I thought that it was my wife's fault, the arrest. I thought I was doing what was expected and all that was reasonable for me to do. As I will share with you in this chapter, I now believe that a *dedicated* martial artist, in particular, may elicit the "arrest" a significant amount of the time. This is inherent within the time demands of our sport and possibly a result of spiritual or interpersonal laziness.

Regardless of how you deal with this type of situation, pausing to nurture that person or refusing for the sake of training, the emotional atmosphere of an "arrest" affects you. It affects your focus, your ability to concentrate, and to a significant extent it determines whether you perform with a "paralyzing" or "enabling" state of mind. Although we often think that training requires "single-minded focus," I

Focus is a function of integration, not isolation.

have learned that focus is a function of integration, not isolation. Your relationships are a vitally important spiritual aspect of your Total Quality Martial Arts experience.

In the overview to these chapters on the spiritual dimension of martial arts, I stated there is a dysfunction if there is not an atmosphere of mutual satisfaction in your relationships. If someone has essentially been forced to "arrest" your attention as you were going out the door, this clearly demonstrates to you that this is an area of life that requires spiritual attention. If it didn't, an arrest would not be needed.

Importance of Relationships

The people who comprise the relationships of your life are crucial for a number of reasons. For one, when they are an affirmed segment of your existence, they support your training and any competitive pursuits. It might be in emotional, physical, or even financial ways. However, they are not just utilitarian considerations.

It is important for you to nurture these people simply because they are people; fellow human beings who perhaps by birth (parents, siblings, and children) or by choice (spouse, friends) have become an irrevocable part of your existence. They have the same basic human needs as you. As such, you play a vital role in meeting their needs and helping them to become actualized—just as you desire for yourself.

> **If we equally emphasize relationships as well as our martial techniques, we can demonstrate a spirit that says, "At a laugh, children draw near, but at a frown, wild animals flee."**

I have watched and read of athletes in the martial arts and other sports who have discarded people for the sake of their single-minded focus on winning. The movies and sports commentators always seem to herald their spartan efforts as somehow being more excellent than people who lovingly attend to their relationships.

Instead, let's marshal our Total Quality resources to be multi-dimensional and fully spiritual. If we equally emphasize relationships as well as our martial techniques, we can demonstrate a spirit that says, "At a laugh, children draw near, but at a frown, wild animals flee."[3] Now that is a martial artist!

Win at All Costs?

Single-minded athletes pay a price for discarding their relationships. Some go on to win but then find that they have no one with whom to share the victory. Some lose or become injured and find they have irreparably severed their relationships and are unable to resume them from the point where they last trampled on them. And sadly, still others find they are able to go on through injury, loss, or victory without any relationships. But as aging sets in and the opportunity to compete vanishes, they find out much later in life that they will spend their elderly years in complete loneliness.

"Single-minded focus" can be a very dangerous thing. Some athletes find that if they don't have a minimum amount of meaningful human interaction on a daily basis, they have trouble with very basic functions such as sleeping. Still others discover that while neglecting people does allow "focus," the energy for that athletic event diminishes over time because the attention it receives has become unbalanced and inordinate. Thus it becomes a task instead of a renewing activity.

If you find yourself blaming other people for your performance or resenting their demands on your training, you must realize that you will continue to be miserable as long as you keep complaining. Once again, you cannot "wish" that these relationships would get better so that you can perform; you must choose to nurture them in such a way that your "arrest" at the front door is not necessary.

Relationship Dynamics

To be part of a healthy relationship, you must participate in a loving manner. Just as the movies have suggested that fulfilling our vocation is quick and easy, the movie images have equally implied that love is effortless; that it just happens. Nothing could be further from the truth.

In the beginning of any relationship, whether with a friend or in a romantic sense, love is somewhat "easy." In romance, once a mutual attraction has been recognized between two people, both find an initial period of time where there is a certain eagerness to find out all that one can about the other. Compound this with the fact that most people only show their "attractive" side in the beginnings of a relationship, and you will begin to believe that this is how the relationship should (or will) be forever.

But interpersonal history has shown that this is not possible. When emotions eventually subside, the real business of love begins. And this reality is a part of all types of relationships. Consider the parents who were so excited about the new baby and then, ten years later, are guilty of child abuse. Consider the romantic couple who were criticized by their parents for quitting school so that they could marry. Now, years later, they sleep in separate bedrooms. Or, how about the friend with whom you were inseparable; going through all twelve grades together and yet now you have not seen each other in twenty years. What is it about "love," in any relationship, that leads to these pitiful situations?

Fundamentally, we misunderstand love. Not only do we see it as effortless, we also see it as something for our benefit. We "love" a person because of how they make us feel. With this perception, when that person no longer makes us feel the same way, we act in hostility or passively drift apart like the previous examples.

Love Defined

Scott Peck has defined love in a way that practically guarantees we could never find a reason to sever a relationship with another person. He defines love as "the will to extend one's self for the purpose of nurturing one's own or another's spiritual growth." Now that's a spiritual definition worthy for martial artists.

Within this definition, you may well consider the benefits you are deriving from a relationship. But to judge its healthiness or vitality, you would not only look at what you are receiving but what you are providing. That is why it would be almost impossible for you to sever a relationship. Within this understanding, a failure is not someone else's fault. It's a shared responsibility.

Relationship Inhibitors

And so we go back to the beginning of this chapter. Is it really your spouse's fault that he or she needed to arrest you at the door and demand attention? Or, is it really because you have ignored them and their spiritual growth which has led to this cry for help? How do you as a Total Quality martial artist assess this situation in your spiritual perspective?

Remember the elderly people who defined their last years in the context of a golf score? Peck terms this behavior "active laziness." Passive laziness, the type we usually think of, expresses itself in literally refusing to do anything, e.g., the "couch potato." But "active laziness" is more subtle, and hence, more pernicious.

Let's return to the example of the martial artist who can't get out the door because he or she has neglected their relationship. As a spiritual person, this athlete has two very basic responsibilities: work and relationships. But what if this athlete does not like his or her job? This athlete could find another job, or, take on an absorbing avocation such as the martial arts that consumes considerable attention to avoid facing the reality of addressing an employment situation.

If married, this martial artist also has a responsibility to maintain their marriage. But in the course of years, this athlete has "grown apart" from his or her spouse. Deep inside, he or she realizes that some reading, some study, maybe some counseling is necessary. But rather than face the poignant silence of the evenings with the spouse, this martial artist decides that training at the *dojo* is necessary every night. This athlete is not in love with the martial arts. This athlete is actively lazy. Training for several hours is easier than exerting the interpersonal effort necessary to improve his relationship.

The Total Quality Assessment

Perhaps at this point you realize that you have used martial arts to be "actively lazy." Perhaps you also realize that the relationships of your life are very important to you for no other reason than the fact that they are your relationships. And from a practical point of view, perhaps you realize that as long as these spiritual stains are part of your life, your performance and focus will be affected. What do you do? First of all, you must be absolutely honest with yourself and within the relationship. The first aspect of this honesty asks why you really are a martial artist and what you reasonably believe will result from it.

As a general rule, the end purpose of your activity will largely determine how your spouse, parents, or friends will react to your martial art lifestyle (in terms of inordinate time or money). If you can show them objectively why you believe that there is a potential payoff, such as a local win, amateur title, or even professional career, they will tend to be much more accommodating. An objective demonstration may allow parents to feel better about transporting an underage driver to the *dojo* at night or to out of town tournaments. It may convince the spouse that there is a chance at making money from this avocation.

This is not to suggest that you shouldn't be a martial artist simply for its own fun and enjoyment, regardless of results. But if you are, and your destination is exclusively amateur, don't try to adopt the spartan lifestyle of a professional in terms of time, money, or focus to the exclusion of your relationships. What is the point? Or is it a case of active laziness?

Secondly, relationships and the individual people who comprise them are all unique. What a spouse in one marriage wants from the (martial art) partner may not even occur to the spouse in another marriage. Therefore, it is not appropriate to suggest an itemized list of specific things that you should do to meet the needs of your particular relationship.

Improving Relationships

Instead, to improve, you need to commit yourself to the basic method that will enable you to find out what your relationship needs to avoid being arrested at the door: communication and dialogue.

If you have a strained relationship, don't automatically seek the advice of your friends or some "sage." Simply communicate. Since love's expression is to seek the spiritual growth of another person, then that is who has the key—that person. It is not a book and not friends; it is that person. It is not a huge mystery. Ask and you will find out. If you will sit down and communicate; if that other person can sense that you are giving them your full attention—if you listen with an open mind—that person is going to share things with you that, if adopted, will restore vitality. Chuck Norris observes that this "means slowing down and opening up . . . listening to all they're saying instead of trying to reduce their concerns to a problem that can be briskly solved."[4]

There is probably a big surprise in that type of spiritual communication. If a person has been unsuccessfully attempting to get your attention for a period of time, he or she has probably levied a whole host of "wrongs" you have committed; so many, in fact, that you think the expectations are overwhelming and unreasonable.

Don't Be Defensive

But this "listing" is more of a method than a factual content. When someone is trying in vain to get your attention, he or she will frequently "escalate" the list of wrongs in an increasing attempt to receive a reply. Being ignored, their anger will grow and thus the growing list of wrongs. This is an opportunity to use your martial arts skills. As an example, you can deflect the anger by not responding in the same manner and thus avoid a confrontation.[5]

> **Your willingness to give your attention allows their spirit to open up.**

Then, once an ignored person senses that you are genuinely listening with the intent to act, the anger will subside and the "list" usually becomes only two or three basic things that the person needs in order to have a sense that the relationship is vital and growing. Your willingness to give your attention allows their spirit to open up. Indeed, communication between two spirits is neither overwhelming nor unreasonable. In a relationship where each person is concerned with the other's spiritual growth, these true needs are usually few, and vital.

The same could be said about the "street confrontations" of martial arts. If you read the stories of some masters such as Gichin Funakoshi, you will see that masters have been able to disarm conflict by communicating with their adversaries. The assailant may be full of rage but a calm spirit and non-defensive attitude caused the assailant's spirit to open up and the rage was dispelled. Do you see the connection between the spiritual aspects of martial arts practice and your personal relationships?

And so, this is your invitation to Total Quality success: establish communication. To embrace the practice of communication, you must first set the precedent by seeking what that person needs to feel good about you, not what you need to feel good about them. This is not to suggest that it will only be a one-way street. It is a reciprocal process; once that person senses you're truly listening and willing to act, he or she will be encouraged to do the same for you.

Communication Steps

In establishing communication, certain practices will establish a conducive atmosphere. Several appear in Stephen Covey's *Seven Habits of Highly Effective People*.[6] These include:

SPIRITUAL COMPONENTS

1. **Do not listen with the intent to reply.** Martial artists who have been accosted for spending too much time training may have a tendency to only listen long enough to launch their justification about the amount of training time. This will not promote communication but escalation of the argument instead. Listen to learn.

2. **Seek first to understand, then to be understood.** In developing your spiritual maturity, you should take primary responsibility for the relationship. This means that you should first seek to understand what is troubling your partner. Once your partner feels understood and affirmed, you can share your feelings to be understood as well.

3. **Do not listen autobiographically.** This is a cousin of listening with the intent to reply. A martial artist who is accosted by his or her spouse about spending more time with the family may say "my mother didn't ask my father for that type of such and such." In essence, this person may patiently "listen" to the partner's grievances, but once given an opportunity, describes their own interpretation of the interaction instead of recognizing the emotions of the accoster. Do not answer emotions with words; answer emotions with affirmation.

When making yourself vulnerable by opening up for communication, if true communication occurs, you will probably hear some things that will not be pleasing to you. In fact, if you feel that you have been trying hard to meet the demands of the relationship, you may feel that the needs your partner is expressing have ignored your good efforts and intentions. This, in turn, may cause you to become angry.

It is extremely important to recognize that anger is not a wrong emotion, either on your part or the partner's. Anger, in an of itself, is no different than any other emotion like crying or laughing. What you must avoid in your communication process is dysfunctional anger, which is when you move from describing what you feel to blaming and judging.

In other words, if your partner shares something with you that hurts your feelings, it is entirely appropriate to say "That statement makes me angry because I have done . . ." By making an "I" statement, you are taking responsibility for your feelings. On the other hand, it is dysfunctional if you say "You would make a statement like that because you are unappreciative and stupid." It is no longer an expression of how you feel, it has become a tool (or medium) for you to belittle your partner.

Suspend Certainty

Peter Senge[7] takes this process of communication within relationships a step further. He describes this fluid process of exchanging feelings and ideas between people as dialogue. In Senge's approach, you must fundamentally render respect to the person you are listening to. To truly respect their feelings and communication, you must suspend your certainty. If you are sure that you are right before, during, and after the communication, regardless of what is expressed, the communication is unilateral. If certainty is suspended, if you are willing to change based on what you hear, then communication has moved to an even higher level called dialogue.

When relationships are strained, it may be difficult to remember what it is about that person that initially attracted you. These memories and realizations may be clouded by your own hostility. But many times, we begin a relationship with a person because we respect their way of thinking and perceiving things. Stephen Covey states we should say, "If a person of your intelligence and competence disagrees with me, then there must be something to your disagreement that I don't understand and I need to understand it. You have a perspective that I need to look at." This type of respect will guarantee dialogue.

How About You?

Are you a martial artist who has been arrested at the door? Do you have relationships that need your attention? If so, accept these needs as your spiritual responsibility, a crucial component of Total Quality Martial Arts. Besides the basic sadness of torn relationships, your performance will be affected. Moreover, you will not find that your performance will increase by neglecting these relationships. As stated previously, focus is a function of integration—of accepting your whole life, not isolating it.

I am certainly not saying that these things are easy to do. I experience both success and disappointment in my attempt to practice these things in my life. Yet just as it may take years to perfect a martial art technique, these relational traits take sustained effort to see the fruits of your personal investment. Remember, even after a martial art technique is "perfected" it doesn't mean that you will perform it flawlessly every single time you use it. There will be lapses.

If your relationship needs improvement, there is no short cut around communication, and that will take sustained effort. When you see a person in one of your relationships hurting, you may be tempted to try and bandage it; a hurried birthday card to a parent, a movie with a spouse, a ballgame with a friend. If these activities are mutually agreed-upon in your relationship, fantastic. But if they are your unilateral attempt to postpone the process of listening, be careful. If you deal with the symptoms of a bad relationship, the core problem has not been addressed and it will repeat itself. To root it out, to nurture that person and nurture yourself at the same time, enter into dialogue. It should be remembered that this dialogue is not just for romantic relationships. That type is often mystified.[8] Dialogue will enhance your relationship with your instructors, fellow athletes, teachers, parents—any human relationship.

The Opposite of Spirituality is Illusion

At the beginning of this second section I quoted Scott Peck to state that true spirituality means living in accordance with an unseen order of things. In these last three chapters, we've looked at your "unseen order" expressed in terms of your potential, work, and relationships. If you don't look at these topics of your life with a practical, value-based type of spirituality as I've described, you could be caught in an illusion that will leave you mystified indefinitely. For instance, you could continue nurturing thoughts of becoming a national champion when your muscle fiber type indicates otherwise. Or, you may believe that all your work and relationship problems will disappear once you achieve "enlightenment" or *"satori"* and so misdirect your efforts to an elusive goal that leaves those areas stagnated.

A Personal Example of Illusion

During my early 30s, I decided that the best integration of all my experiences, preferences, and talents would be to become a special agent with the Federal Bureau of Investigation (FBI). Like most people in our society, I viewed the FBI almost mythically in it's self-description as the premier law enforcement, if not overall governmental agency, of the United States. The illusion induced a deep response in me.

As soon as I applied, I began a training program that was nothing short of exhaustive. Physically, I began a battery of isometric exercises to meet the FBI's standards for push-ups, sit-ups, and pull-ups. Because a prospective applicant film showed Quantico trainees boxing, I went full-tilt in martial arts training. Despite my dislike of running, I reached the point where I was doing one hour endurance runs along with sprints on the track. Because I thought I could be "called up" at any time, I never let my devotion wane and ran through two winters. I literally ran sprints on snow covered outdoor tracks.

But my training was more than just physical. To prepare myself mentally, I read dozens of books on the FBI to learn about their culture and history and made lists of notes from those books so that I could be conversant on FBI topics when I went to Quantico. I also read every newspaper article on the Bureau so that I knew what cases they were involved in and, again, made laborious notes so that I would have ready recall in case a topic came up later in my training or service as an agent. I interviewed current and former agents to learn how certain ethical situations should be addressed by a good agent and memorized the Federal hierarchy of the Department of Justice and the congressmen and senators whose voting would affect FBI affairs. I bought a pistol to enhance my marksmanship and even took my family through a Total Quality "selection grid" process to determine what duty station we would select as our geographical preference. In short, I pulled out all the stops. I sought to train and educate myself in every manner conceivable so that I could become a respected agent.

After finishing the application process and receiving a tentative date to attend Quantico, I was suddenly dismissed from further consideration by the Bureau due to an arguably negligible medical problem. I was crushed. I had invested nearly two years of preparation. When I talked to other prospective applicants, they acted nonchalant about their preparations if accepted. I had trained my will, my body, and my mind to a peak for service as an agent.

As the realization of the dismissal settled in, I began to realize the role of illusion in my pursuit of the FBI position. On the one hand, the FBI had failed me. But on the other, I had failed myself. In the months following the disappointment, I realized how big the issue of competency was for me. Although it's obviously good to prepare ourselves for life's tasks, I was seeking recognition beyond normal competency. I wanted to land at Quantico with a bang and be recognized as the premiere trainee. Why else would I have run intervals in the snow and ice?

But even more significantly, I realized that I was seeking a huge illusion regarding the FBI itself. Because they were considered premiere, I now realize that I was subconsciously asking the Bureau to give my life a sense of meaning that I wasn't experiencing in my own (non-FBI) work. In other words, I wanted them to make me feel good. To take away the bad feelings or dogwork associated with my current career. This was an illusion. It is the same type of illusion that prompts us to think all will be well once we achieve a certain belt level or win a tournament.

We should start to suspect an illusion when we have to disregard conflicting information about our thought processes. Although the Bureau's public image was suffering during my application process due to Waco, Ruby Ridge, the Montana standoff, "Filegate," and the premature arrest of the Olympic bomber, I either dismissed those incidents or thought that once I was in I could change things. When the administrative process for becoming an agent became eerily similar to the same types of bureaucracies we're all familiar with, I refused to think they could be anything less than their elite image. I was anxious to become an agent and disregarded those aspects that didn't match the image of the Bureau. But again, this wasn't so much about my faith in them as my desire to escape the present and receive recognition as a special agent.

Besides selective screening, we should also suspect an illusion when we think that something will change how we feel about ourselves, how others perceive us, or how we deal with unsavory experiences. I wanted the FBI to make me feel and be perceived as premiere. I wanted to be part of the myth.

That's why I embraced such rigorous training methods of my will, mind, and body.

As martial artists, there is a tendency toward an illusion that the black belt will confer a certain status. If your tradition emphasizes Zen, there may be an "enlightenment" or *"satori"* illusion that suggests detachment as a means of making it through the daily world of work or the unpleasant aspects of your relationships. But just as the FBI cannot give my life a sense of meaning I'm not otherwise willing to develop myself, the illusions of becoming a national champion or mystic martial artist will not address your true spiritual needs.

These needs require personal investment in your work and relationships; the type I have described in these past two chapters. Meeting those goals is not sudden or effortless; they take dedicated, conscientious efforts. What's more, to be truly spiritual means that those areas derive meaning by what you bring to them, not by what they bring to you. I thought the FBI agent experience would confer a sense of meaning on me. In reality, what is before me this very day, from my salaried work to this writing, becomes meaningful by how I practice them—not by what they bring me. Can anything less be considered spiritual?

PART THREE

Creating Our Future

INTRODUCTION

*"We think in generalities but
we live in detail."*
—ALFRED NORTH WHITEHEAD

Some people and businesses make themselves so successful they fail. Single-minded focus on success at the moment (or even in one year) can leave us paralyzed with regards to the future—a dynamic that is unfolding in every present moment. It is similar to financial planning: we must spend money to meet our present needs but save as though we'll live for several more decades. If we spend too much now, we'll suffer in the end. If we focus only on the end, we deprive ourselves now. To be successful, we must think in sufficient detail about the present as well as the future.

In a shift from the physical and spiritual concerns outlined in the Part One and Part Two, I now turn to how we create our futures. This includes ourselves, our martial arts community, and in the public's perception. In Chapter Eight, we'll examine how we create our own individual future for ourselves with a "Portfolio"—the sum of all our choices and strategies. In Chapter Nine, we'll look at what we should consider doing for our fellow martial artists if we want to flourish—or just survive—in a "business as usual" manner. And of utmost importance, in Chapter Ten we'll examine our perception in the eye of the public—a factor we can't overlook.

Seneca said "in a moment the ashes are made, but a forest is a long time growing." Let's plant the seeds that will create a forest-like haven for martial artists for generations to come.

CHAPTER EIGHT

FOR OURSELVES AS MARTIAL ARTISTS: THE "PORTFOLIO"

"We first make our habits, and then our habits make us."
—JOHN DRYDEN

There is a genuine sense in which any athlete who is committed to his or her sport is an artist. This is particularly true of the martial athlete. You and I are artists. We normally picture an "artist" as someone who creates a painting, or perhaps even a musician. But if we look beyond the mere product, the fundamental characteristics of an artist are the use of skill and creative imagination in forming their aesthetic pleasure. The martial arts ". . . allow a practioner to assume responsibility for what he is, and to claim the just rewards of creative action."[1]

We Are an Artistic Expression

Given a physical body with certain athletic endowments, it is the individual "artist" who uses skill and creative imagination to create the best possible performance. These skills and creative imagination are necessary for athletes in general and amateur athletes in particular. For just as the painting artist has a wide array of colors to choose from in their creation, so the martial artist has a wide variety of subjects and available methods to choose from that affect per-

Martial athletes are artists with many dimensions.

formance. Furthermore, while a professional martial artist will try to use as many resources as possible, the amateur, due to more fragmented time management, must carefully choose which resources to employ.

The variety of resources includes comprehensive topics such as technique and strength training, nutrition, physiology, and competition. Moreover, it is an understatement to suggest that these are huge fields of study. Many people pick just one field and create a vocation out of it. And yet the martial artist, in order to be successful, is responsible to be functionally knowledgeable in not only these fields but in perhaps a dozen more. This takes creativity and resourcefulness that earns the term martial artist.

A professional, who is paid to perform, can exclusively focus on these various fields of performance. An amateur, on the other hand, is normally one who works full time and in many cases has a family as well. Thus, creativity is not just about choosing from the myriad of subjects to be integrated into performance. It is also about such mundane aspects as trying to allocate adequate training time. In terms of time management, the amateur's avocation frequently begins when the professional athlete's vocation ends: at 5:00 P.M.

In turn, what we amateurs need is our own personalized "portfolio," just as a painter has one that shows his or her works of art. Even in simple terms of athletic training, how do we decide what areas to focus on and which areas can be postponed? We do this by clearly identifying our vision, articulating an objective that realizes the vision, and designing effective strategies to move us from where we are now to where we want to be in the future. These three components become our "portfolio." Below, I discuss each component in detail, and what you need to actualize them.

I. Vision

The first segment of the portfolio is vision. Before and above all things, a martial artist must have a vision, or mental picture of what he or she wants to become. Peter Senge has noted that most adults don't have personal vision. Instead, when asked about "vision" adults will frequently answer with what they want to get rid of—not what they want to become.

How many times have you heard the hypothetical question, "What would you do with a million dollars?" In adults without vision, a typical "quit work; lay on the beach" is the characteristic answer. On the other hand, if a person described something like starting a new business, that would be considered an active vision. If the million dollar question prompts you to describe the things you would quit, your answer is more about retreat than vision.

How, then, does this apply to the martial artist? If asked by their instructors, I suspect that most martial artists would say their "vision" is either a black belt (or the next higher rank) or to win at a tournament. However, in terms of a true vision, I suspect both of those answers are flawed.

I state this about the black belt because the United States has an extremely high attrition rate of martial athletes who earn a black belt and then stop training. Apparently, these persons have that static view of life I alluded to previously. In contrast, many noble statesman of the martial arts consider the first degree black belt as only the beginning of the real journey into the deeper aspects of technique and self-mastery. If a "vision" only compels you to a certain point in time then it is more appropriately termed a short-term objective, not a vision.

Winning is not a true vision, either. It is a relative measurement (as I demonstrated in Chapter Four) and may well be outside of your control. A true vision should largely be within your realm of influence.

• An Illustration of Communicating Vision

There is an illustration among organizational business trainers that illustrates the effects of true vision. It goes something like this:

Two fireman from the same department are to present a fire safety demonstration to elementary age children. In introducing their topics to two different classrooms, the two firemen use completely different approaches. The first introduces his subject by standing and stating "I am here today to talk to you about fire safety." With this introduction, this fireman's audience continues to doze. The second fireman introduces his subject by stating "I want to tell you a story about a boy, a puppy, and a box of matches."

The second fireman's audience is engaged! The use of these "word pictures" stimulates the audience's imagination and causes them to give their full attention. It is so much more natural and motivating to relate to a mental picture, or vision, than it is to mere words. Your vision as a martial artist must be equally motivating to yourself and to the people in your life. It should not be static or based on circumstances outside of your control.

• My Personal Vision

Like anyone else, I like to advance in belt rankings and win during competition. But as I've just outlined, these are flawed substitutes for true vision. In its purest sense, a vision should be a mental picture that exceeds yourself. In my own personal portfolio, my vision as a martial artist is to facilitate "a learning community comprised of fit martial artists seeking their own and other's development." By emphasizing a learning community, I can still have intermediate "visions" (more accurately, objectives) such as advanced ranking or winning in competition. But if those things don't occur, my world is not crushed because my vision exceeds myself and what I individually achieve. The vision is to see the martial arts community at large become a learning community that enables other people's development.

Not only is this purer than "winning," it is also enduring. My vision doesn't stop if I cease competing. Since the emphasis is on a learning community, it will continue endlessly. You need a vision like that.

II. Objective

The second component of the portfolio is fairly simple and direct. Objective. What do you have to do in order to see your vision realized? Since my vision is to foster a learning community, my objectives are to maintain my own skill and fitness levels, model desired behavior, and share learning points about training matters that help develop fellow martial artists.

III. Strategy

The third and final component of the portfolio is strategy. This describes how you will perform to meet your objectives and realize your vision. Since my vision is a learning community and my objective is to share learning points, my strategies are created by determining how I believe I will most effectively see those first two components realized. That is one reason why I pursued certification as a Specialist in Martial Arts Conditioning—to understand sport science that would help develop martial artists. So far, the most effective way I've found to do that is to write articles in magazines. Writing, then, is my strategy.

Of course, a particular strategy may change. With the emergence of the Internet, I may find that is a more effective strategy to see my vision realized. Or perhaps audio-cassettes that martial athletes use while driving in the car to minimize "dead" time. The particular method is not set in concrete. The important point is that strategy answers "how."

- *Selecting Strategies*

In creating a vision, you are a martial artist by use of the imagination. In developing and using strategies, you are an artist by use of your skills. Some of these skills are already well developed. Others still need development. If you were previously unaware of systematic training but now see how it could be useful to you, study of this subject may now become a strategy and part of your portfolio.

The Total Quality Martial Arts approach emphasizes that the total amount of factors affecting performance and the individual should be addressed (e.g., technique, lactate and aerobic conditioning, flexibility, absorption, measurement, and spirituality). However, due to the complexity and volume of any given subject compared to the amount of time any of us have available, the selection of choice becomes a critical matter of selection. Since there are so many topics and fields of study, a martial artist, whether professional or amateur, cannot individually achieve a deep knowledge in all these fields. An example:

In creating your portfolio you may determine that strength training is definitely a desired emphasis for the upcoming year. You may also determine that writing about what you discover in strength training should be part of your portfolio. As you'll discover, the topic of strength training is a huge field of study. So is the art of publishing! Do you have the skills and time necessary to do both? You don't necessarily have to, even if they're both strategies, if you use "strategy tiers."

A strategy tier is categorizing your needs and want's into three lists. Just as an understanding of physiology helps you interpret what types of training you should perform, this method of prioritizing helps you interpret which tasks you should pursue, which you should ignore, or which should be fulfilled in an alternative manner. It also helps meet the conflicting time demands of two very desired skills—such as studying strength training—and then publishing articles about them. To create your portfolio, develop an "A," "B," and "C" list of those topics that are a part of your life as a martial artist in particular and as a human being in general.

- ### *Strategy Tiers—The "A" List*

To determine your "A" list, go back to the first two segments of the portfolio, vision and objective. In my case, my vision is to create a learning community and my objective is to share information, I will then choose the activities that I believe are most likely to reinforce those elements. For example, when I go into a bookstore, there are dozens of authors who write that I must perform their training program or I will not be effective. What's more, an atmosphere of fear is created when the authors state that every other successful martial artist is practicing that recommendation. How do I know which book to buy, then?

I can pick up a book that will show me how particular techniques are effective in competition. And these are quite often detailed studies. Yet another book may describe how strength training will make just a few techniques more effective than possessing an "arsenal" of techniques. Which book should be on my "A" list? The one that I most reasonably anticipate will help meet my objective—in my case, the book on strength training because I believe we're better off performing a few techniques well than a hundred in mediocre fashion. In part, I base this assertion on the opinion of Bruce Lee who stated a handful of well-mastered techniques serves a martial artist better than 100 techniques half-learned.[2]

Essentially, the "A" list comprises those activities that are most closely connected to your vision and should be non-negotiable. If pressed for time by work or other responsibilities, these "A" list items are those things that you absolutely will do regardless of the circumstance. If you scheduled lactate and aerobic training on a Thursday evening but worked late and can only do one or the other, as a Total Quality martial artist you will choose the activity that is most needed in the current development process. Again, this will be up to the individual. Use of the "A" list allows you to prioritize among conflicting training and life demands.

- ### *Strategy Tiers–The "B" List*

The "B" list comprises those activities that you believe are beneficial but not absolutely necessary for your performance. In most cases, the "B" list contains potential "A" list items, at least in terms of your interest. You would like to do such and such, and probably will when time or perhaps money allows. But if a choice is required between lactate and aerobic training on that Thursday evening, the realization that you have "wind" but are lacking intensity tells you that lactate training will be the activity. They are both viable training aspects, but one is not as important as the other.

• Strategy Tiers—The "C" List

The "C" list comprises those activities that you know are an aspect of performance but which hold minimal interest to you. For me, the "C" list is history. I am generally bored by the standard introductions to how the martial arts began in distant countries thousands of years ago (I accept their existence and enjoy what's occurring now). But, I also recognize it is an important subject. So what do I do? In my portfolio, I interact with martial artists who have history on their "A" list! It can take hours to read history and comparisons among different systems. Hours that I am not interested in and would rather spend conditioning. But if I can hook up with someone who enjoys this reading, that person can give me a synopsis in a matter of moments that I can use in my next article or seminar. As "payment," I can perhaps share some of my "A" list related material with that person who finds my interests on their "C" list.

• Strategy Tiers for Life in General

This approach to discerning your strategies is tremendously beneficial for your overall life as well as your practice of the martial arts. Let's continue with that example of the scheduled lactate and aerobic session on Thursday evenings. On a particular Thursday, your parents are coming in from out of town and the lawn must be cut before Friday night. It's currently one hour before the lactate training. Whether you skip the training to cut the lawn depends on your list.

One option is to put the lawn on your "B" or "C" list and perhaps contract it out! Pay that neighborhood kid to cut it, or perhaps trade services. Ask your neighbor to cut it in exchange for cutting his or hers in the next rotation. In Total Quality Martial Arts, we must accept the fact that each of us creates our own reality. Avoid excuses. It will not do to say "I couldn't do lactate training because of the lawn." And, try not to wait until the last moment so that a crisis decision has to be made. Whether you do lactate training or not is your responsibility—your created reality.

Responsibility

All too often, martial artists cry out that they cannot perform how they want because of external forces (such as the lawn). This is simply not true. Within your genetic ability group, you perform exactly how you want.

Spiritual reality teaches us that you will always do exactly what you want. You may verbally say that you don't want to cut the grass and therefore miss lactate training. But what you really want is to avoid the embarrassment of having an overgrown lawn. That is what drives your decision. In this example you can do it yourself which, in this "crisis" mode, reveals where lactate training is on your list. Or, as an artist who creates your own portfolio, you can pay to have it done and therefore accomplish both needs. This addresses responsibility and the use of strategy tiers.

> The habit of blaming something external will perpetuate submaximal results.

You can say that you want to train more effectively, but if you are unwilling to purchase quality training equipment, what you really want more is to hold on to your money. You see, whether you train effectively or not, you always get what you really want. There is always some trade-off, some choice that may be hidden to those around you but which has been more attractive to you than top performance.

The reality of choice underlines the act of creating a vision, objective, and strategy. In our choices, there is both a revelation of what our priorities are and an opportunity to create those priorities. What's more, the will becomes stronger each time it's used.[3] Our reactions to circumstances (we didn't know our parents were coming in until the last moment) reveals our priorities and what we really want as martial artists. If we use circumstances as excuses, they become part of a powerless paradigm that will be discussed shortly. You must, therefore, take responsibility for creating your performance. The habit of blaming something external will perpetuate submaximal results.

Instead of blaming or excusing yourself from training, become active and take responsibility for a personally created portfolio. Don't shy away from the martial arts because all the topics necessary for performance appear overwhelming to you. Enlist others who can help you become familiar with a vast array of information. Use the Internet. Don't settle for the back of the pack because your work, spouse, or home responsibilities are precluding training time. Pay or trade services with someone to do those things that are consuming your time whether it's yardwork, laundry, or vehicle maintenance. Develop your strategy tiers.

And most important of all, recognize that whatever state your current portfolio is in, whether you have clearly identified objectives or ineffective strategies, you have created the portfolio. If you don't like it, you have the power to recreate it. It is yours. A portfolio is the sum of all your choices and strategies.

Developing Your Mental Potential

In the discussions of potential throughout this book, we have reviewed the raw, genetic, physical potential within athletes. This examination shows that an athlete may not genuinely compete against just any other athlete. To line up a genetically elite athlete against a normal athlete means boredom for the elite and overload for the normal. While a martial artist with a predominance of Type IIB muscle fibers would have very fast, powerful kicks, he or she may not fare well in a kickboxing competition where more fatigue-resistant muscle groups are necessary.

Assessing one's potential is like understanding the fuel capacity of a vehicle. A person would be deemed foolish to state, "I'm filling up the tank and driving from New York to California." First, you must know how many gallons of fuel a particular vehicle holds to determine if it is truly possible to make it from one point to another considering the vehicle's capacity.

Likewise, you must know which destination is most individually suitable for you before mapping out a course of action. This "mapping" begins with assessments such as temperament testing, elite comparisons, and muscle fiber analysis. Once you understand these aspects of potential, you're then ready to begin mentally achieving potential. In other words, taking the mental and psychological steps necessary to see all your potential realized regardless of the caliber—national, regional, local, or simply within your own *dojo*.

Once you objectively determine a "destination," the final component is your psychological suitability for the task. Let's assess your mental skills needed for your objectives in a couple of ways. First, I invite you to complete the Mental Profile that I've adapted from Joe Friel.[4] This well help you determine any specific mental skills you need to develop. The assessment is fairly self-explanatory. Answer each question by indicating how you would characterize yourself on a scale from 1 to 6. When you've finished the assessment, you will be able to determine if you need any mental skills development in the assessed areas.

Mental Profile

Read each statement below and choose an appropriate answer from these possibilities

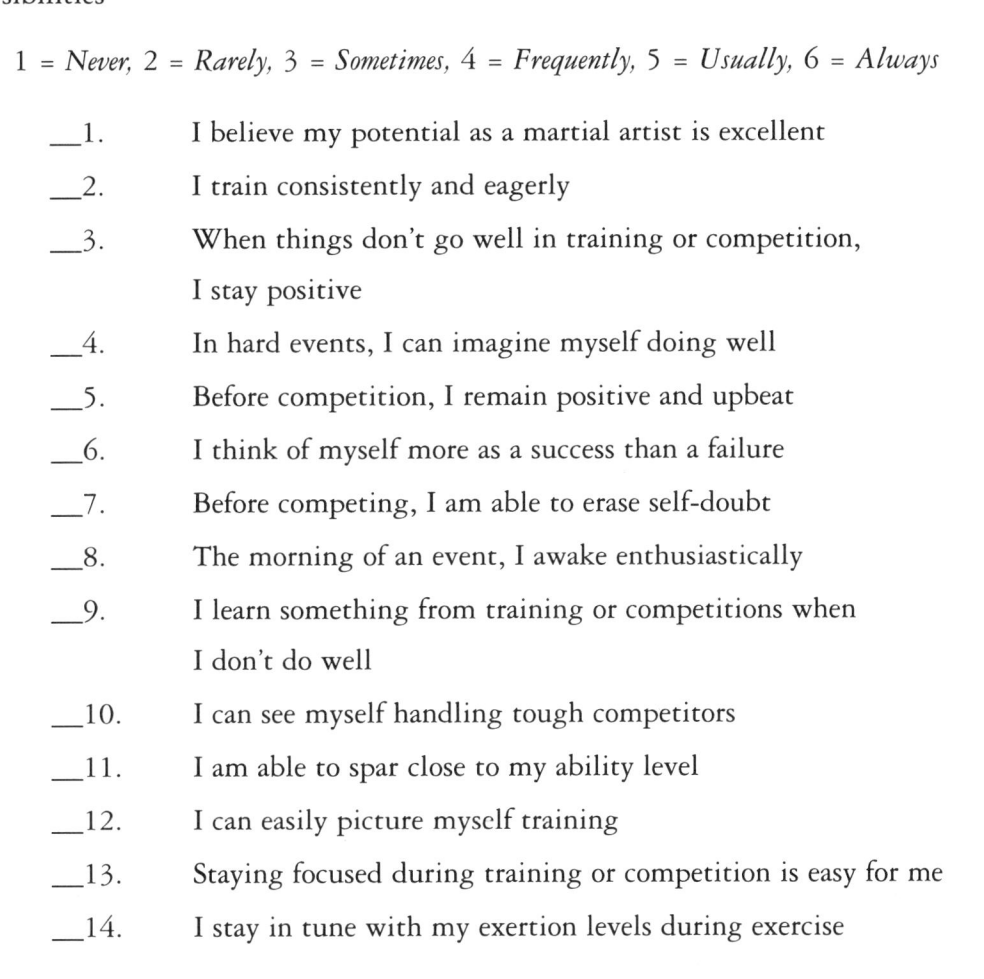

1 = *Never*, 2 = *Rarely*, 3 = *Sometimes*, 4 = *Frequently*, 5 = *Usually*, 6 = *Always*

___1.   I believe my potential as a martial artist is excellent
___2.   I train consistently and eagerly
___3.   When things don't go well in training or competition, I stay positive
___4.   In hard events, I can imagine myself doing well
___5.   Before competition, I remain positive and upbeat
___6.   I think of myself more as a success than a failure
___7.   Before competing, I am able to erase self-doubt
___8.   The morning of an event, I awake enthusiastically
___9.   I learn something from training or competitions when I don't do well
___10. I can see myself handling tough competitors
___11. I am able to spar close to my ability level
___12. I can easily picture myself training
___13. Staying focused during training or competition is easy for me
___14. I stay in tune with my exertion levels during exercise

___15. I mentally rehearse strategies before competition

___16. I am good at concentrating as a match progresses

___17. I make sacrifices to attain my goals

___18. Before an important event, I can visualize doing well

___19. I look forward to workouts

___20. When I visualize myself in my martial art, it almost feels real

___21. I think of myself as a tough competitor

___22. In competition I tune out distractions

___23. I set high goals for myself

___24. I like the challenge of a tough competition

___25. When the match gets hard, I concentrate even better

___26. In competition, I am mentally tough

___27. I can relax my muscles before rigorous training or competition

___28. I stay positive despite late starts or bad referee calls

___29. My confidence stays high the week after a poor tournament placing

___30. I strive to be the best athlete I can be

• *Scoring*

Add the numerical answers you gave for each of the following sets of questions:

Motivation:	Questions 2, 8, 17, 19, 23, 30:	Total: ___
Confidence:	Questions 1, 6, 11, 21, 26, 29:	Total: ___
Thought Habits:	Questions: 3, 5, 9, 24, 27, 28:	Total: ___
Focus:	Questions: 7, 13, 14, 16, 22, 25:	Total: ___
Visualization:	Questions: 4, 10, 12, 15, 18, 20:	Total: ___

Now, your collective answers have measured your mental skills in five critical areas. The scoring for these results is as follows. Do any of the results suggest some emphasis on your part to fully develop mental potential?

Total	Ranking
32–36	Excellent
27–31	Good
21–26	Average
16–20	Fair
6–15	Poor

In addition to the assessment and what it might reveal to you, let's look at a couple of other aspects that might be otherwise overlooked in this important consideration.

Self-Beliefs

The first step in your mental journey to realize potential requires an assessment of your self-beliefs. Quite often, it is the self-beliefs that determine the winners in genuine competition among groups of similarly talented athletes. We've all known "achievers" and "underachievers"; those who seem to maximize their genetic gifts and those who seem to fall short of their potential within a given ability group.

Sometimes these performance shortfalls are the result of purely physical variables such as inadequate training or poor nutrition. If you have sound training that addresses the physical components and still are not fulfilling potential, then the possibility of an internal problem such as self-beliefs is possible.

Consider an example outside the martial arts. American bicycle racer Andy Hampsten placed fourth in the Tour de France (the cycling world's premier event) on two occasions but was unable to win. In 1989 he stated that "As much as I try to prepare, something always goes wrong." Do you believe that his performance will override his belief? What do you believe about yourself? Do you believe that "something will always go wrong?"

Powerlessness

Theorist Peter Senge identifies two performance-contradictory beliefs that may prevent us from realizing our potential and achieving what we really want. The first belief is powerlessness, a passive attitude that often expresses itself in phrases such as "I am unable to achieve because of . . ." The second belief is unworthiness; an almost unconscious belief that we don't deserve our dream. I realize that as you first see these two words you'll say, "No, they don't apply to me." But consider the following example.

In an approach similar to Senge's, psychologist and author Michael Durst[5] states that powerlessness is often expressed in what he terms "automatic behavior responses" (ABR). If a problem is some other source's responsibility, then we may feel justified to stay in our current problem state.

If we blame any source outside ourselves, we've empowered that source.

In terms of spiritual growth and mental achievement of potential, we're confronted with this reality: if we blame any source outside ourselves, we've empowered that source. In other words, whatever we blame apparently has more power than we do. This is the attitude of powerlessness. Since a martial athlete, and especially an amateur, has other responsibilities in life, it may well be true that work, family, or school affect training and performance to some extent. But if we want to achieve spiritual maturity and reach potential, these factors must be considered opportunities instead of problems. For example, these "problems" may be candidates for the strategy tier exercise I previously outlined.

Unworthiness

The other performance limiting belief can be a sense of unworthiness. For reasons that may stem from childhood or other lifetime experiences, some athletes are actually more afraid of success than failure. Durst states this is because the achievement of success could actually contradict one's self-beliefs.[6]

Beliefs about who you are and what you are capable of within a given ability group are imposed limitations that you have made rea-

Have you given yourself permission to succeed as a martial athlete within your ability?

sonable, or agreeable. Tell an achievement-oriented martial artist they can't test for their next belt and they will reject your statement; they believe that contradicting their desire is unreasonable. But once a person accepts a belief, whether positive or negative, an internal process has been performed that makes the belief reasonable, or agreeable, to the believer ("Maybe I don't deserve the belt"). Durst states that "the only difference between you and the president of the company is that the president has given himself or herself permission to be president and you haven't."[7] Have you given yourself permission to succeed as a martial athlete within your ability?

New Self-Beliefs

If beliefs of powerlessness or unworthiness characterize your self-beliefs, a new set must be created if spiritual maturity and top performance are to be achieved. One of the best sources for creating new beliefs is the gifted author and speaker Anthony Robbins. In his books *Unlimited Power*[8] and *Awaken the Giant Within*,[9] Robbins provides dozens of methods that allow the willing athlete to change performance-paralyzing mental attitudes into an enabling state of mind. One method is termed "Neuro-Associative Conditioning" and is brilliant in its simplicity. Here is a breakdown.

Anthony Robbins and others offer methods for creative new mental pathways.

1. Decide what you really want and what is preventing you from having it. This may require an intensive inventory.

2. Create leverage—assign pain for not changing and reward yourself with pleasure for changing.

3. Interrupt the limiting pattern (the limiting behavior or attitude).

4. Create a new, empowering alternative.

5. Condition the new pattern until it's consistent.

Simple, right? But how many people, or athletes in particular, exert the discipline necessary to sit down and commit themselves to the thought and follow-through that will bring new results? John Stuart Mill said that "one person with belief is equal to ninety-nine who have only interests." Beliefs are the foundation of all behavior. No one commits a single action that is not believed possible whether a daily task or athletic feat. So, in order to reach your potential, whether as a local amateur, national champion, or professional martial artist, you must, in the words of Robbins, "reinvent yourself by systematically organizing your beliefs and values in a way that propels you in the direction of your life's design and potential."[10]

By working with thousands of people, Anthony Robbins has demonstrated that if you truly desire to begin the process of actualizing your potential, you must realize that it is your decisions, not the conditions of your life, that determine your destiny. And the core decisions necessary are those that involve your self-beliefs. Robbins states that "making a true decision means committing to achieving a result and then cutting yourself off from any other possibility." How committed are you to the full realization of your potential? Enough to aggressively stretch your self-beliefs? Mediocrity is not measured between elite and normally gifted athletes but by the extent to which your genetic gifts are developed.

A Final Note on Mentally Achieving Potential

In Total Quality Martial Arts, potential has been examined in both an objective and a subjective sense. For the sake of your spiritual health and the mental welfare of those with whom you interact, it is in your best interest to assess yourself objectively with the MBTI temperament assessment and against certain physical standards such as muscle fiber type, VO_2 max, and the characteristics of elite kickboxers.

Among martial artists within your "genetic pool," it is your individual responsibility to identify and use all the ethical resources available to perform within your capacity. In the relative sense of competition, a large degree of your success depends on your subjective beliefs about yourself.

Draw close to the conversations of many athletes and you will hear them say "I wish that I could do such and such." In pursuing your potential, remember that to wish is passive; to choose is active. This is the final touch in creating your individual portfolio.

CHAPTER NINE

FOR THE COMMUNITY OF MARTIAL ARTISTS: CHOOSING TO FLOURISH OR SURVIVE

> *"Service is the rent we pay for Living."*
> —MARIAN EDLEMAN

If you think broadly about the martial arts—that you're interested in seeing them grow and not just your own experience in it—then you have probably experienced some frustration at what is both phenomenal and volatile. The martial arts are phenomenal in that somewhere around 30 million people world-wide practice the arts with four million of them in the United States. This is double the estimates that were made by noted thinkers such as Bruce Haines who, in 1968, predicted two million U.S. practitioners by the turn of the century.[1] Moreover, we are a $1.5 billion dollar enterprise that has doubled in growth since 1990.[2] This is particularly phenomenal considering that the vast majority of these athletes are not professionals and accept rigorous training and the inherent injuries of a contact sport.

Furthermore, an estimated 1.5 million people start out in the martial arts every year. But like the amount of schools that disappear overnight, the "stick" factor is obviously missing. If that 1.5 million stayed, the population of the martial arts community would be staggering. But it's volatile, with a lot of turnover, and less than 10% of beginning students making it to the second degree black belt level.[3] Whether you are an instructor trying to make a decent living, or simply someone who likes to have a lot of peers to practice with, this volatility can be frustrating. So how, then, can we serve our community of martial art enthusiasts by growing in a sustainable manner?

Based on my experiences as an author and coach, along with the research I conducted while earning a masters degree in marketing, I propose that sustained growth is possible by embracing three important principles: values, technology, and sport science. Let's look at each one and their implications.

I. Values

Some of the most visible representatives of martial arts are very well-meaning but off-target in contemplating how to grow the martial arts community. Many believe the future of martial arts resides in youth, the "right people," or educational, grass-roots programs in the school or community. Still others think it's about practicing successful business principles (such as salesmanship). One national coach articulates the problem as ". . . we don't have a corporate sponsor. Until we get that corporate sponsor, the sport isn't going anywhere. It will stagnate. It's got to be marketed or promoted."[4]

While each of these aspects are a component of growth, they are not the core ingredients and never will be. In particular, the idea of "marketing" is usually synonymous with advertising which is not what true marketing is all about.

• *Marketing Defined*

In classical marketing terms, a product-oriented business attempts to sell the virtue of the product to the consumer ("You should buy this knife because it's the best"). This "sale" is for the benefit of the seller, not the buyer, and is expressed in advertising and promotion. In contrast, a market-oriented business creates and meets the needs of the consumer ("If you need something to cut meat with, I'll make you

> **We're in danger if we focus on the martial arts instead of martial artists, the people, and their values.**

Professional marketing consultation can help create sustainable growth.

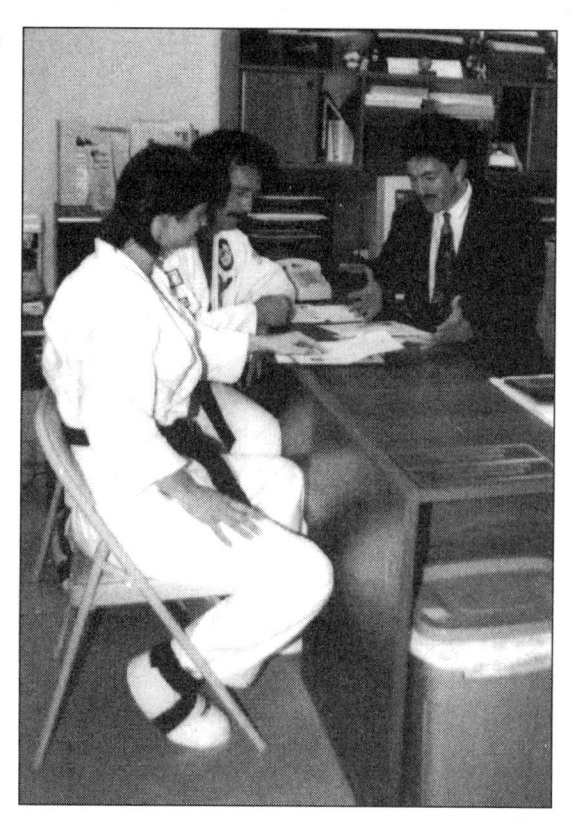

a knife"). Instead of a "sell," this is an exchange. Primarily, the consumer's needs are met. Secondarily, someone profits financially.

There is a classic marketing example to illustrate this difference between product and market orientation.[5] At the turn of this century, a wealthy Boston millionaire saw his mission as providing electric streetcar use. Upon his death, he unintentionally sentenced his heirs to poverty by stipulating that his entire estate be forever invested exclusively in electric streetcar securities. You see, instead of focusing on the market need (transportation), he focused on the product (streetcars). If his will would have stipulated exclusive investments in transportation, his heirs could have adopted to the changing times. But the inflexible product emphasis ruined his intentions. If we're not careful, we're in danger of the same error if we focus on the martial arts instead of martial artists, the people, and their values.

Read the perspectives of the most visible representatives in the martial arts and you will almost always see the same "organizational enhancement" themes (education, grassroots, sponsorship). The problem is that these are insular themes that are designed to improve the (martial arts business) organization—but these aspects are not capable of meeting the values of martial artists in a true marketing sense. To grow in a sustainable sense, we must meet those values—just as the Boston millionaire needed to meet transportation values. In turn, we don't secure sponsorship to attract martial artists, we attract sponsorship because we have so many martial artists. The "stick" factor in sustaining the amount of martial artists that attracts sponsorship lies in meeting primary values.

• *Primary Values*

My marketing research of the martial arts reveals that while self-defense skills are strongly desired and often the catalyst in drawing new students, they are actually a secondary concern to more strongly felt values. The real primary values include convenience and psychological improvement.

As part of my masters degree thesis research, I discovered that an overwhelming majority of new students choose a martial arts school based on con-

Improved self-confidence is the largest perceived benefit of martial art instruction.

venience. In terms of transportation, the average student travels only 1.5 miles for instruction. This finding was reinforced by other research of parental observations and school age karate participants which noted the primary reason for choosing a particular martial arts program among boys was convenience.[6] Thus, in a strict business sense, these two research elements reinforce the familiar emphasis on "location, location, location" in addressing the growth of martial arts.

It is also important to note that the definition of convenience should not be restricted to how far a student drives for instruction. The martial arts are also convenient in the sense that equipment costs are minimal, it can be practiced individually or in a group, and it's an activity the whole family can practice together. Try to discover all the ways the martial arts meet the value of convenience and you'll unlock one of the keys to sustainable growth.

- *The Second Primary Value*

We can all see the basic wisdom of location and convenience regarding instruction. But we must also ask what prompts students to enroll in a program in the first place? Is it self-defense?

The same research that demonstrated the primacy of convenience also indicates that the majority of new students desire psychological improvement even more than self-defense skills. Specifically, new students (or their parents!) desire more self-discipline, assertiveness, and self-confidence. In fact, 83% of the parental observations stated improved self-confidence was the largest perceived benefit of martial arts instruction.

But how do we respond to the need for sustainable growth? Do we focus on convenience and psychological improvement? Almost never. We talk about education, advertising, and promotional practices like students are fish waiting for the right bait. Or, less business-savvy but equally earnest instructors often feel they must emphasize skill development in themselves and in their students to preserve traditional values and promote numerical growth. All time and energy is spent refining skills to contrast themselves with "hollow" instructors.

The truth is that physical fighting (or fitness) skills are really only a medium through which we all achieve feelings of satisfaction and improved self-confidence. Whether martial arts or school sports, successful physical activity improves mental outlook and that is a primary value for martial arts students. Just emphasizing the skills is only half of the matter. Competency is always of paramount importance, but successful marketing of martial arts is not just about skills. It's about the primary values of convenience and psychological improvement. Once these values are met, aspects such as education and sponsorship come naturally.

- *Applying Primary Values for Numerical Growth*

In regard to convenience, this means more than just the careful consideration used in selecting a site for a new school. In terms of comprehensive marketing efforts, locational convenience helps define channels of advertising and promotion. As a business example, if you want to distribute flyers, they may prove effective if placed on windshields within a couple of miles of your school. If handed out at a tournament where the participants are not within your "radius," the effort may not bring any substantial results.

Since the estimated average age range of martial arts students is from seven to 16 years old, convenience should be emphasized to create growth. For example, what are some ways to provide instruction for people too young to drive? Immediate, after-school instruction is a relatively untapped market. How about coordinating with your local school district to have buses drop off students at your school? This would prevent the "latch-key" syndrome and allow parents to pick up their children on the way home from work instead of a separate round trip at night. (Remember: convenience!)

If busing is unfeasible, try providing instruction at the school gymnasium after school. The same after-school and parental transportation benefits exist for both the students and the parents. The marketing possibilities are endless if you focus on the customer's needs for convenience. And, don't forget that since the majority of the martial arts community is between the ages of seven and 16, the mother is often the primary decisionmaker in both enrollment and in the ongoing costs associated with practice. We must learn to think of what's convenient for her!

Videos and CD-ROMs help address other aspects of convenience. Just because a student isn't at the *dojo* six nights per week doesn't mean he or she isn't committed to practice. Other demands, such as school, work or family, may preclude that type of attendance. Rather than judging a student or fellow athlete as "uncommitted," try to develop or access in-home means of instruction and motivation to help meet the need for convenience. Look at the proliferation of in-home, self-study college and vocational training.

Once growth is created through convenience it must be sustained. To meet the second primary value, think of ways to promote increased feelings of psychological improvement. This could mean a written annual evaluation of performance. I suspect that a mentoring program where senior students actively reinforce the efforts and accomplishments of the newer students is one of the unrealized resources for sustainable growth. The decision to quit an activity is almost always made in isolation without a positive, reinforcing support network. Sustainable growth can also result from the simple act of consistently making direct eye contact and sincerely stating "good job" to students eager for affirmation. You must remember that new martial artists primarily choose a program because it's convenient and stay because of increased psychological self-improvement. The lack of perceived self-improvement accounts for the relatively stable population of the martial arts community, despite how many beginners try it out every year.

• *Values First*

I realize there are some compelling arguments for establishing education, good business practices, and solicitation of sponsorship to attract and grow the martial arts community. While these may result in some short-term positive results, I don't believe they have the same forcefulness as meeting core values. Do we need sound education and standardized instruction? Yes. But those aspects don't cause students to "stick," they refine techniques and enhance the organization. Do school owners need to know how to handle a prospective client that states he'll have to ask his spouse about joining? Again, yes. But making the sell and keeping the student are two different things. And, could we use a few million dollars in Olympic sponsorship? Obviously. But did Michael Jordan play great to receive Nike sponsorship or did Nike sponsor him in order to play great? He played great first. In the same way, we must grow our community by consistently meeting primary values so that the total population of athletes compels sponsors to seek us out. These values are convenience and psychological self-improvement. Fulfilling those values comes first in the dynamic cycle of growing our community in a sustainable manner.

II. Technology

Technology not only changes cultures, it also defines the competitiveness and vitality of businesses and other activities in every generation. In this day and age, the most visible technological change is the computer in general and the Internet in particular. An estimated 150 million people "surf" the Internet and users are growing at an estimated rate of 15 to 20% per month.[7] What do these people do on the Internet? They buy, sell, trade, and access tons of information. What can the martial arts community do on the Internet? Perhaps distinguish itself as a cutting-edge enterprise full of ideas and innovation.

On the Internet and World Wide Web, users can play in many ways. One is called "on-ramp" access—looking up information that's posted on a "bulletin board" about certain topics. For instance, to learn about resistance train-

Sensei Howard High is an exceptional instructor and Internet innovator

ing, Internet users can use a search engine and type in the topic to find hundreds of authoritative articles and commentary on the topic. I call this on-ramp access "static" because a user is referencing posted information—sort of like the old card catalogue at libraries. Once linked to the Internet in this manner, you can be connected to martial artists in 38 countries around the world.

On the other hand, there is also "virtual" access available where users can "talk" real time with other users, such as the "chat rooms" featured in America Online (AOL). Pioneers in the martial arts community such as Michael DePasquale, Jr. of *Karate International* magazine are creating information havens featuring this virtual access. Beginning in September of 1996, DePasquale's "Martial Arts World" became the largest single access source for martial arts education and entertainment.

But there are extremely useful applications at the local level as well. Howard High of Overland Park, Kansas maintains an exceptional web site (http://www.jkr.com/kansas) for use by his current students as well as prospective students. The site includes school information such as the calendar of events, class schedule, tuition rates, requirements for testing, and frequently asked questions.

Is this useful to our communities? It's not only useful, it may well determine which schools and instructors are still around five years from now. At the local level, instructors waste an enormous amount of time by answering individual questions at the *dojo* instead of assuming primary responsiblity for instruction. Wouldn't it be better to have prospective students check out a web site which is available 24 hours per day instead of the few hours a school is open?

At the national level, innovations such as "Martial Arts World" features directories on broad topics such as self-improvement, self-defense, references, and training. Once in these directories, a user can find all types of information that will help distinguish us as a learning community—not just enthusiasts who emphasize traditions.

Through the Internet, you can learn how to treat injuries, design training programs, research nutritional needs, or find out what types of violent crimes plague a certain city. Essentially, you can discover all the information available on any topic a whole lot quicker and with considerably less effort than the old method of going to the library. It can also be used simply for fun such as finding out about your favorite martial arts movie star or downloading graphics. There are literally hundreds of WEB site locations with information that will keep you abreast of the most recent developments in the martial arts. For an introduction to existing martial arts web sites, check out the article by Wilson Goodson listed in the References.[8] If you'd like to create your own, Sandra Wakai offers a concise summary of the necessary steps.[9]

• *Equipment Needs*[10]

To seize the benefits of this technology, you'll need to purchase or have access to a computer. To begin with, you'll need an 040 (Mac) or a 486 (IBM) for the central processing unit (CPU) with 16MB RAM to meet basic Internet e-mail demands. If you want to go virtual, such as the "Martial Arts World," you'll need a Pentium CPU and 28.8 digital fax modem in order to stay "real time" and download graphics without falling asleep at the keyboard. In addition to these tangible equipment pieces, you'll also need browser software for the Internet (such as "Netscape") and, of course, an Internet provider. America Online is currently your best option if you want to use the martial arts chat rooms.

• *The Internet Keeps You Current*

The purchase of a new computer system with these capabilities can be around $2,000 for a new system or perhaps $1,000 for a used system. While this may exceed your immediate capacity, you should look at these costs in several ways. For one, what is the value cost of not participating in the Internet? You not only miss out on the most recent developments in martial arts and sport science, you're behind the power curve in advertising and communications if you're interests are professional or business-related. Even as a non-professional athlete, you may find yourself talking about the best way to deliver a sidekick (as explained to you 20 years earlier) while someone else, connected to the Internet, is learning about the best training methods to deliver the sidekick. The difference? Information and access to it. Technology causes that difference.

III. Sport Science

For our community to grow in self-respect as well as public perception, we need a total commitment to sport science. I outlined some of the introductory aspects in Chapters One and Two concerning energy systems, muscle fibers, and training components. In Chapter Five we reviewed objective means of assessing potential. It is this and much more that we must embrace if we are to establish the credibility that other sports have established for themselves.

In other words, we can no longer rest on anecdotes (traditions and training myths). It is easy to empathize with sincere instructors who do not realize that hitting the bag 90 times in two minutes will compromise maximum power. But it's simply inexcusable to perpetuate myths like advocating endurance running for point sparring.

If we want to generate the same respect that other sports receive, we cannot allow ourselves generalized thinking or "leaps in logic" regarding our training. For instance, I once read an advocate of practicing without shoes state that shoeless training increased the torque generated in the pivot of kick. But the context of the comment was in regards to street self-defense! That type of faulty logic is too often characteristic of training approaches. We can no longer remain ignorant of what type of resistance training is necessary to develop endurance versus power, what level of endurance is needed for our martial objective, or whether someone actually has a chance of becoming an elite martial artist. With the science that's available, there's simply no excuse.

- *Cadre Training*

What every martial arts school (or pocket of practice) within the larger universe of all athletes needs is a cadre of trained specialists in the martial arts. Individual *dojos* should consider sponsoring the study of martial art sport science so that the fundamentals are available to all practioners. This requires a change in the paradigm of how we view the martial arts. Instead of looking at the head instructor as the single sage of all knowledge regarding technique and training, we must realize that we must all contribute to the growth of our community and that means that more than the head instructor must be knowledgeable. It is too much to ask of one person and it is the very antithesis of community to expect it. In a community, everyone participates for the common good.

• *Football Analogy*

There is not a single head coach in professional football that personally supervises all aspects of training and performance. What we see is a cadre of coaches with various specialties such as special teams coordinator, quarterback coach, linemen coach, and so forth. And this is for perhaps 60 players. With average enrollments of 200 students, how can we expect one person to know how to develop all those different types of martial artists? We must approach the martial arts like the professional football team coaching cadre. We all have a role.

For instance, some students can contribute their accounting expertise to the ongoing success of a school. Others, in the context of this discussion, can specialize in the various components of training. Several students can specialize in flexibility, nutrition, anaerobic conditioning, and still others in resistance training, just to name a few of the components. Then, as certain questions arise and training programs are contemplated, different individuals will contribute to the overall growth and success of the school. It is okay for an instructor to turn to a junior student and ask "what do you know about the subject," when asked a question he or she is unfamiliar with.

> **The old paradigm of one-instructor-master-knows-all is inappropriate for today's martial art community.**

The old paradigm of one-instructor-master-knows-all is inappropriate for today's martial art community—especially with regard to sport science. Once you begin to review the technical principles involved in matters such as energy systems and muscle fibers, you'll realize that even just one component can make a lifetime of study and work for the interested student. It's simply not possible to know all things.

Trying to rely on the "master" can also be a form of dependency that numbs our own curiosity and growth. Former Chicago Bulls coach Phil Jackson states that one of his biggest obstacles was to overcome the team's reliance on Michael Jordan.[11] Under pressure, they expected Michael to bail them out. Under the master-sage paradigm, we're vulnerable to the same tendency as martial artists. We shouldn't expect our instructor to do all our homework for us; we need to study and conduct some research on our own. Then, along with the instructor and our peers, we can become a learning community instead of simply learning by rote.

As I mentioned at the beginning of this book, the two best sources for researching sport science at this time are the International Sport Sciences Association (ISSA) and National Strength and Conditioning Association. The ISSA has a program of certification specifically regarding the martial arts and the NSCA offers the broad sport science principles relevant to all physical activities. Furthermore, each one meets the criteria of this chapter: they offer the value of convenience through in-home study and are available through the Internet.

• *How Science Can Prevent Misunderstanding*

Sometimes you just don't understand why—you've trained hard, ate right, and rested well. And yet at the dojo, you've felt weak—laboring for breath after a few mere rounds of sparring.

Is there something wrong with you? Not necessarily. Your frustration could be due to the indoor air at the *dojo*. Specifically, it could be because of the elevated levels of carbon dioxide characteristic in relatively small areas of space where many people are exercising.

You see, the science needed to grow our martial art community applies both to ourselves and to the physical environment that surrounds us. If we're ignorant of the muscle fiber or enzyme types, we can train incorrectly for years. If we don't understand the very nature of our contemporary *dojos,* we can cause unnecessary frustration among ourselves. As an example, martial artists frequently have difficulty exercising in crowded rooms that were not designed to accommodate physical exercise. This is due to those elevated concentrations of carbon dioxide.

• *CO vs. CO_2*

To begin with, let's ensure we understand the differences between carbon monoxide (CO) and carbon dioxide (CO_2). CO is the type that comes from automotive tailpipe emissions. CO_2 is "emitted" by humans and animals as part of the respiratory process, especially during intense exercise. Our natural respiratory process seeks to maintain the proper concentrations of oxygen, carbon dioxide, and hydrogen ions in our tissues. When we exercise, pressure in our cells causes carbon dioxide to be transported from our cells to the lungs and exhaled. In fact, when you see a 100 meter sprinter doubled over, it's as much to get rid of carbon dioxide as it is to inhale new oxygen.

When a group of people get together for indoor exercise such as the karate *dojo,* massive amounts of CO_2 are generated in a small amount of available air space. In turn, the very thing our bodies are trying to dispose of are present in levels of high concentration.

• *Effects of CO_2*

Carbon dioxide is an "asphyxiant" which means that it interferes with the availability of oxygen for the tissues. Furthermore, CO_2 dilutes or displaces oxygen in air and creates levels of inadequate oxygen required for normal function. If you exercise in an indoor area where CO_2 is rapidly removed, no problem. But many *dojos* are converted storefronts where the ventilation system's air

Converted storefront dojos often have inadequate ventilation for martial athletes.

exchange rate (ACH) has not been created with exercisers in mind but instead sedentary consumers. Air exchange rate is the rate at which indoor air is exchanged with outdoor air each hour. This could answer the question of "why me?"

• *More on Air Exchange Rates (ACH)*

During the past couple of decades, building construction has featured decreasing ACH rates because of an increased desire for energy efficiency. In other words, building owners want decreased operating costs incurred with their ventilation systems. In many buildings today, the exchange of indoor air with fresh outdoor air is as low as 0.5 per hour. This means that the volume of air inside your *dojo* would not be replaced in its entirety for two hours (one half the total volume per hour, 0.5). Why is that a problem?

Excess CO_2 is an inhibitor of performance. If insufficient oxygen is available due to the "scavenger" effect of CO_2, lactic acid is formed. Normally, lactic acid accumulations that increase breathing and hinder muscular contractions occur at perhaps 85% of maximum heart rate in well-trained athletes. But if the air in your *dojo* has high concentrations of carbon dioxide, excess lactic acid production could occur at only moderate rates of intensity, such as 60% of maximum heart rate. You could be particularly vulnerable to this, for example, if your *dojo* runs consecutive classes hour after hour: you may be walking into preexisting high levels of CO_2.

• *"Try Harder!"*

Some well-meaning instructors see a student laboring for breath and think the student simply isn't training hard enough. In fact, the student (you!) may be trying too hard in an environment that won't support your efforts. Various environmental studies have shown that indoor concentrations of some contaminants are often two to five times higher than outdoor concentrations.[12] This is due to that air exchange rate discussed earlier. Wherever you're sitting right now has certain levels of CO_2. But if you're sitting in a 8' x 8' room, think of having three other people jumping in place and try breathing that air after a while. It's ripe with CO_2. It is like the experience of being inside a cardboard box.

Exhaustion may have more to do with the facility than the level of training.

• *How You'll Know*

The normal percentage of oxygen in air is 21%. Levels below 19.5% are considered unsafe. If you're in a small workout space with a lot of people exhaling CO_2, you may experience symptoms including headaches, drowsiness, heaviness in the chest, an abnormal increase in respiration rate, and decreased ability to perform strenuous exercise. If you or your peers are experiencing these symptoms you may need to take action. Particularly if your workouts away from the *dojo* seem fine but those inside seem unusually strenuous or trigger these symptoms.

• *What You Can Do*

First, take a look at the amount of people trying to exercise inside your *dojo*. Are your classes trying to cram 50 people inside a 1,000 square foot facility? This could overload the air exchange rate ability of the building and either endanger you or inhibit your performance. If your *dojo* frequently has a lot of people in a small space, you and your instructor should consider restricting the *dojo* time to an emphasis on practicing technique and not so much on exercising at aerobic and anaerobic levels.

Second, your *dojo* class should open the door or any windows available to let the excess CO_2 escape. A little longer break between classes would also help decrease the levels of CO_2 generated. Plants absorb CO_2 from air and will also help but this process doesn't occur quickly enough to accommodate perhaps 60 people over a three hour period.

Third, your *dojo* should consider purchasing a hyperoxic (oxygen enriched) breathing machine for emergency situations. This is that mask with 97% pure oxygen that you see NFL teams using when they visit the Denver Broncos at Mile High Stadium.

If your *dojo* is in a well-ventilated area, this CO_2 problem may not apply to you (you do need to train harder!). But, if you are in one of the many *dojos* that are in converted storefronts with inadequate air exchange rates, the most cost-effective and training-efficient method for you may be split workouts. If possible, perform your intense exercise in well-ventilated areas (preferably outdoors) in the early morning or late evening. This will enable you to avoid exposure to harmful outdoor contaminants, such as ozone, which peak during the middle of the day.

Remember that while you want to avoid outdoor contaminants, concentrations of inert gases such as CO_2 can be two to five times higher indoors so there is no panacea in either realm (outdoors or indoors). Considering the relative exposure risks (midday ozone versus high indoor CO_2), outdoor exercise in the morning or early evening is probably the best compromise and is one-half of the split workout recommendation. The other half can be in the *dojo* with an emphasis on technique training that means excess levels of CO_2 won't be generated.

Please note that I am certainly not suggesting that karate classes should not be intense in nature. However, intensity should be managed intelligently. If there are a lot of people in a small space and students are experiencing symptoms like those discussed, some steps have to been taken to protect health. It might be managed as easily as opening doors and windows and then it's okay to be intense as a group. Or, if the building won't handle it, the group may need to go outdoors for certain parts of intense exercise or use a split-training program as just described.

Do you see how important the role of sport science is? Without understanding this underlying reality, you could doom students or yourself to unwarranted judgements about your ability or conditioning. Science is the pathway out of that harbor.

Keeping a Perspective on "Growth"

This chapter has outlined essential ingredients for sustainable growth among ourselves as the martial arts community. We can flourish by embracing values, technology, and sport science. As demonstrated here, these principles encompass considerations that are important but regrettably neglected by martial artists. Some are subjective like the psychological needs of students. Others are objective like the indoor air that can limit our performance no matter how intelligently we train.

Addressing and implementing these principles takes a sense of service to our community. If we believe in ourselves and our collective potential, we must be willing to accept new approaches. In another decade, it may be time to discard those ingredients in favor of even newer ones. That's the dynamic nature of life expressed in *kaizen* (continuous improvement). Or, we can just survive, content with our 10 person class at the YMCA rehearsing the same traditions that we learned a couple of decades ago. Each of us must decide what we want to carry in the portfolio of our created future.

Are we willing to come out of our comfort zone? For some, that means trading in an hour of television viewing time to learn about the Internet, or perhaps studying for a fitness certification. For some instructors, it may mean willing to leave the comfort of a mental model that says "I must know all" and ask students for help in understanding the complex subjects involved in training and physiology. Conversely, students can't exclusively rely on their instructors but must be willing to conduct research on their own—both to verify what has been stated by the instructor as well as to help the instructor answer questions posed in class. This is service that will grow our community.

It is important that we view growth as more than numerical increases or revenue. While I have a sincere desire to see sustainable, numerical growth and want to see instructors and other types of professional martial artists support themselves, growth should not be defined by just the amount of spectators or corporate sponsorship available but by the martial artists themselves. For it is always the martial artists themselves that make the martial endeavor superior to other types of physical activities and our community worthy of itself.

For example, how many professional football players would continue to incur the physical demands of the sport without their high salaries? Yet martial artists practice just as rigorously, incur similar types of injuries, and, in the majority, do it for free. And this has been the practice by millions of people for approximately 2,000 years. In a real sense, this demonstrates that the martial arts grow despite the volatile population numbers. It could even be argued that it has outgrown it's original purpose and context (unarmed combat for military and civilians) yet been maintained for all these years. Thus, even if we have minimal spectators and a moderate corporate presence in the form of sponsorship, we know we must have something of real value to endure in this manner. How we fare in the future will depend on how we address the primary values, technology, and sport science.

CHAPTER TEN

IN THE EYE OF THE PUBLIC: ENHANCING OUR PERCEPTION

"A pessimist is someone who has to listen all the time..."
—ANONYMOUS

It should be our goal as a community to be held in the highest regard possible among the general population. This does not mean the overall public must like the martial arts, but we should generate enough respect to be viewed favorably in the public's perception. This should be our goal because if we are not highly esteemed, or if we are scorned, than we are in jeopardy of losing our rights to practice. We could risk reverting to ancient times when the arts were practiced in secret. Does this sound far-fetched?

Examples of Poor Public Perception

In 1996, a young "Toughman" contestant died in an amateur combative match. The response? Due to the efforts of the young man's mother, the Governor of Missouri banned all forms of combative fighting in the state, excluding certain types of "sanctioned" events such as professional boxing.[1] Since then, several other states are reportedly using the Missouri law as "model legislation" and preparing bills of their own to outlaw combative fighting. Sound familiar?

Also, in 1996 the United States Congress considered similar legislation concerning "ultimate fighting." In 1993, a massive marketing campaign was initiated to protest Teenage Mutant Ninja Turtles as obstructing literacy in school-aged children (the premise being that children were focusing on kicking one another instead of reading). And in my own marketing research thesis, almost 40% of all surveyed people thought of fighting when they heard the term "martial arts."[2] Like the lingering effects of the professional baseball strike, we have a perception to overcome if our community is to flourish.

Should We Advocate the Martial Arts?

When trying to shape public perception, interested people normally engage in what is called "advocacy," an articulation of the parties interests which usually go along the line of ". . . we have a right to . . . (abortion, equal pay, drug usage, etc.)." As any casual observer can see, this type of advocacy usually results in friction. And one of the foremost reasons for this friction and stagnation may well be attributed to the advocacy approach. To "advocate" inherently means to argue; to assume that one's own position is right and the other's is either wrong or uninformed. I therefore suspect that this assumption within advocacy efforts could partially explain the friction between any cause and the general public. Assuming one's position is right and attempting to force another party to that position based on "rights" establishes an atmosphere of "advocacy," otherwise known as an adversarial relationship. This approach, by definition, does not attempt to build consensus, and even raises resistance in the party receiving advocacy efforts.

Advocacy Redefined

Just as true marketing must be understood in the context of the customer's values, so true advocacy must be understood from the public's perception. In other words, it's not enough to state that the martial arts promote "discipline, self-confidence, and coordination" as seen in so many Yellow Pages ads. The public must understand that there are benefits for them—whether they personally practice the arts or not—by the existence of the martial arts community.

Bill Wallace seminars demonstrate how humor enhances learning and probably advocacy as well.

To accomplish this, we as martial artists must identify some form of a benefit analysis that goes beyond conceptual arguments such as our rights or improved motor skills. The U.S. Surgeon General issued a 278 page report in 1996 that states nearly half of Americans between the ages of 12 and 21 are not vigorously active on a regular basis,[3] which is linked to the mortality rate. Since the martial arts are vigorously active, what can we do with that information?

As a hypothetical example, let's assume an insurance company reports that $100,000 of health insurance expenditures are saved through every 50 people who exercise. In your city, estimate the total population of practicing martial artists with these figures and then calculate what the total savings might be in your city. Remember, this means that premiums are reduced for both exercisers and non-exercisers alike. This is what would be communicated to the general public who wonder why they should care about the martial arts community.

As a real example of quantitative savings, the National Institute on Aging (NIA) conducted a study and determined that elderly people who practice tai chi chuan are 60% less likely to fall and break (brittle) bones. Since falls by the elderly account for an estimated 12 billion dollars in medical and disability bills,[4] that means the estimated annual cost could be reduced by perhaps 3.5 billion dollars if half of the elderly population practiced tai chi chuan. Now that is something to advocate!

In less quantitative but equally compelling research, psychological studies have conclusively demonstrated that martial artists are less hostile, have decreased anxiety, an increased sense of responsibility, and are more socially intelligent than their peers who don't practice the martial arts.[5] So why should the public care? Because we as a community represent increased physical vitality and social stewardship that benefits the public! It's not just our "rights"—it's to their advantage.

An Example from the Bicycle[6]

Historically, the bicycle was always resisted by non-cyclists for one reason or another. During the late 1800s, it was resisted by people who owned and rode horses because of how the horses became spooked by an oncoming cyclist. Later the bicycle would be resisted by saloon keepers because active cyclists weren't drinking as much; by theater owners because cyclists were engaged in active recreation; and by organized religion because cyclists were missing church for Sunday rides. And these are but a few examples of the resistance that has always existed in one form or another.

Much of the successful integration of the bicycle into public use during debates like that with the horse owners was the result of organized advocacy groups like the League of American Wheelmen (LAW) in the late 1800s. (Incidentally, LAW is now known as the League of American Bicyclists as of April, 1994). By increasing their early membership from 50,000 to one million members, LAW was quite successful and all Americans owe a considerable debt to this organization who lobbied for paved roads and increased recognition of the bicycle.

Many current advocacy groups look to success stories like that of the early LAW activities as a model and attempt to use a formula of "increase members to increase advocacy voices to raise public sentiment." (This is an implicit assumption in the belief that corporate sponsorship is needed for the martial arts to flourish). In other words, if the lobby or education is strong and persistent enough, the general population will eventually be converted. Or, at least legislation will be enacted. What most current efforts overlook in an example of a group such as LAW is that the effective advocacy efforts were not just a rights-centered approach and a strong argument. In the late 1800s, bicycle advocates first engaged the public in an understanding of the benefits for the whole population from those who rode bicycles.

Early advocates carefully analyzed how the bicycle would benefit the vocations of the doctor, the minister, the postman, and the policeman. For farmers, early advocates printed newspaper editorials with statistics about how many roads were paved within a neighboring geographic region in contrast with the newspaper's region. This served to make the farmers want paved roads in their own region (which was then a benefit for the cyclist as well). For good measure, pictures were printed in the newspaper of farmers with a horse-drawn wagon stuck in the rut of an unpaved road to show what the farmers were missing.

Thus, successful bicycle advocacy in history is really a three-part formula: 1) the desire to ride; 2) how it can benefit those who resist; and 3) advocating with a rationale based on mutual benefit, not just the exercise of a right. Historically, the bicycle was recognized as a vehicle even during the debate with horse owners. But it was not enough to simply demand the rights of cyclists to overcome resistance. Successful advocacy carefully calculated and then articulated the benefits to those who would be infringed by the use of the bicycle.

Our Application

In order for our advocacy efforts to flourish, whether combating legislation or adverse marketing campaigns, we need an approach that demonstrates detailed benefits for the general public. Just telling the public or the government that we have a "right" is a marginal movement at best. Carefully calculating and depicting how our community benefits us all will reduce the resistance and build communication between martial artists and the general population. Consider the process of legalizing casinos and the lottery throughout different states. The proponents have carefully expressed the detailed benefits of adopting these practices for all members of the general public. These benefits are demonstrated as increased funds available for a host of government services including education and increased police forces.

You might start by researching the Surgeon General's report, tai chi study, and psychological study that I referenced earlier in this chapter. These sources demonstrate benefits that you can use to articulate our collective value. You should also consider some browsing on the Internet. For instance, although martial arts are now practiced as a combat sport, martial artists suffer less injuries and fewer emergency room admittances than supposedly safer "organized" team sports. There are many facts on the Internet that are useful for this initiative.

> To overcome negative perceptions among the public, we must help people reframe their thinking.

Overcoming Perceptions

Besides the benefits, there are some definite misconceptions in the public that must be overturned. For instance, non-martial artists frequently believe that we are about violence and revenge. This is probably the result of those frequent themes in the movies that both serve us and endanger us. They serve us in that numerical growth has been directly attributed to martial arts action films and television aimed at children.[7] But the cinema also reinforces negative stereotypes.

If talking to someone who holds these stereotypes, point out that much of modern, sport-oriented, martial art is about exercise and the chance to work out with others. You can also express how martial artists frequently serve the general public by sponsoring anti-drug campaigns and rape prevention seminars with training. You might cite an organization such as the Federation of United Martial Artists (F.U.M.A.) that is dedicated to reducing the incidence of violent crimes. If someone believes that all martial artists are a bunch of "brick breakers," try some humor. State that while learning to break bricks does seem to enhance concentration, most martial artists you know want to break bad habits (like fear and laziness) instead of bricks. To overcome negative perceptions among the public, we must help people reframe their thinking.

Reframing Our Thinking

Of course, the real key to helping the public reframe their perceptions is to reframe our own thinking and paradigms about the martial arts. One important change is the role of the head instructor that I mentioned in the previous chapter. We can no longer consider him or her to be the all-knowing master or sage for all our questions and concerns. We must, again, become a learning community, where every member contributes to the overall good.

And to become a true community, we must strive together to decrease the amount of school closings and high turnover rate in the martial arts. Instead of arguing about which art or system is the best, we should recognize that different styles will meet different people's needs. To serve the entire community, we should direct students to other schools whose needs will be better met away from our instruction. In turn, we can expect that from other schools.

If two schools of different martial art systems are both struggling financially, they should consider consolidating instead of arguing about which is better to allegedly attract new students and stay solvent. This is what I mean by reframing our own thinking. If consolidated, the two schools can share expenses, divide up the facility time, and offer more diversity to the public. That's good business, effective marketing and helps our community perception at the same time. As a whole, we don't receive any "points" when someone sees five different schools open and close at the same location in a five year period. We get the reputation of being flaky. That's a perception to overcome.

Long Term Emphasis

What we're talking about here is not a "quick fix." Perceptions are formed over a long period of time and are often dismantled even slower. Even with your total commitment to the types of positive, benefit-based approaches outlined in this chapter, the change may not be realized in this generation but perhaps the next. But without your commitment, the change will never be realized.

Numerous sports have had similar challenges. Betting, drug use, and fixed outcomes have plagued football, baseball, basketball, and boxing at one time or another. It has then taken concerted efforts to recapture the public's original passion for the sport (baseball is the most recent example due to the prolonged strike and missed world series).

The Challenge of Decentralization

As we contemplate how to create our future by increasing the public's perception, one formidable challenge is the decentralization of the martial arts community. "Decentralization" means there is not a central governing body as in most professional sports. By virtue of the autonomy present in the martial arts, this has tangible effects that all of us feel. For instance, the degree of skill needed for a black belt under one instructor may well be far less than that required by another. A winning technique one week may not even be recognized in another tournament.

Insofar as these differences relate to decentralization, I believe they are acceptable although obviously frustrating for all of us at one time or another. I disagree with the efforts of some who want to establish one governing body over all martial artists for the same reason I object to one governing body for churches: we have different preferences that one centralized system is incapable of addressing. In the words of Peter Urban, "karatemen feel about their practice and style the way religious people feel about their religion."[8] I believe there is no more hope of a unifying governing body over all martial arts than there is of bringing all Protestants, Catholics, Mormons, and members of Islam and Judaism under one roof. We will have, and must respect, differences. Decentralization is inherent to the martial arts. I do agree with Urban's assessment, however, that there can be "unity" for the limited purpose of entering internationally recognized competitive events, such as the Olympics.[9]

I also disagree with the premise that decentralization is the result of martial artists pursuing financial rewards.[10] Profit is an incentive that is useful in many ways. Practically speaking, it allows a full-time focus by instructors to increase their skills and our own.[11] Would you rather receive medical treatment by someone who practices two hours a day or someone whose life is dedicated to his or her profession? By virtue of seminars, tournaments, and other incentive-based offerings, the arts grow in exposure and numerically. Decentralization among martial arts is no more of a problem than our decentralized style of raising families or worshiping in church. It's a challenge, yes, but a problem? Successful leadership means integrating differences, not suppressing them.

On the other hand, when decentralization results in a lack of accountability, such as ethical and financial integrity, that sort of decentralization is bad for our community. Rather than seeking one governing body for all martial artists, even concerning a lack of accountability, I suggest that we seek similar types of influence, or reference, for the matters that govern our practice. For training, we should refer to martial art sport science, such as that offered by the ISSA, to generally guide our decision making processes. We should also consider voluntarily subscribing to the business ethics articulated by an organization like the National Association of Professional Martial Artists.

Decentralization will always be a characteristic of the martial arts. While your school may practice a "kinder, gentler" form of sparring, another school may consider every sparring match the "world championship" and incur the tense, injury-filled atmosphere associated with that type of aggressive approach. Whether it's sparring, ethics, or what constitutes a black belt, the answer doesn't lie in a centralized organization. If you really want to help change other pockets of the martial arts community, go back to the guidance concerning relationships in Chapter Seven. True, sustainable change may be available to those who patiently practice increasing their small circle of influence with people of another viewpoint. The force exercised by a centralized body, like rights-centered advocacy, will always elicit resistance. It's not the answer.

There will always be a certain amount of tension that you'll simply have to tolerate in the decentralized martial arts. But would you really want it to be the other way around? Would you want the standards so rigid on a national basis that individual instructors (or referees) couldn't take individual circumstances into account? That's equally frustrating. Accept the tension.

One of the great aspects of martial arts is that each school has an opportunity to create it's own "garden of Eden." Because all classes don't have to be conducted in the same manner, we can all create—or seek out—the environment that best suites us. We will raise public perception of ourselves when we demonstrate how we can cooperatively work together despite our differences in systems, history, and traditions. Along with the articulated benefits discussed earlier, all these efforts will create and shape our future.

Let's Show an Openness

Remember how I defined advocacy? It inherently means to argue; to assume that one's own position is right and the other's is either wrong or uninformed. Martial artists often have a belligerent and defensive attitude about the superiority of their own system that is both offensive to the martial arts community and the public at large. They, the public, see our "squabbles" and are turned off. If we'd show some openness and appreciation for one another, we might not only find an enhanced perception among the public, but a few benefits for ourselves as well. A personal anecdote that convinced me of the need for martial art cross study might help.

I've never practiced the physical techniques of aikido but that art saved me from a potentially severe injury. It reminds me that we in the martial art community can always find study beyond our own systems beneficial. Perhaps it should even be considered mandatory.

I practice Shotokan karate and train for high performance cycling. On a certain bicycle training ride, my attention wandered for a brief second and I suddenly found myself running into a curb and catapulted into the air. My bicycle and I quickly separated: it went for an unguided cruise while I auditioned for gymnastics.

There was only a brief second in the air before I landed. Amazingly, I watched myself, without conscious direction, initially reach my arms out to brace for the fall. Then, without thinking, I watched myself pull them back in, roll on one shoulder, and land softly on my back. I was unharmed and completely without blemish (except for a stain on my cycling jersey). What happened in that one-hundredth of a second that I pulled my arms back and rolled instead?

When I got back on the bike, I replayed in my mind how I watched myself literally withdraw my arms from "breaking the fall." As I stated, I've never practiced aikido but some recent martial art cross-study learning helped me survive what could have been a serious injury. It was that study that led me to withdraw my arms while in flight.

Only a few days prior to that crash, I was reading an anthology of various aikido instructors. One of them mentioned how people could save themselves from injury if, in his example, they would not try to brake their falls by extending their arms as bicyclists frequently do when they head over the handlebars.

The fact that I only read that example once and never actually practiced it physically is astounding considering how it saved me from a potentially broken arm, collarbone, or worse. I was delighted to escape uninjured. As I reflected on the incident later that evening, it reinforced in me what I am sharing here: there is value in reading and learning outside our own martial art. It's what I'll call "martial art cross-study."

In my system, shotokan, we never practice falling. As with any system, though, there are innumerable nuances to learn in order to become proficient and be considered an "expert." The tendency, then, is to study our respective systems in exhaustive (and exclusive) detail to become as competent as possible. Ironically, our pursuit of competency can often lead to alienation from other martial artists and contribute to poor public perception of ourselves.

Naturally, it is good to seek competency. But we should demonstrate some openness at the same time. If I had only focused on reinforcing my own art, I might be writing these words from a hospital bed instead of an upright position in a comfortable chair. By engaging in "cross-study," I learned something that protected me. In the truest sense of the martial arts, I learned a means of self-defense that literally applied to the street (and how to cushion my fall there!).

Many of the people I know in the martial arts community are so intent on achieving competency they can miss opportunities to learn, and apply, principles and techniques from other systems. And, as my experience demonstrates, the learning might be applied in either a traditional martial art sense or as a matter of course in other areas of life. Since my two interests are Shotokan and riding bicycles, I could have arguably been spending my time strictly doing one or the other. Punches and strikes to develop karate skills. Miles on the pavement to increase aerobic capacity. Studying the instructors, coaches, or racers that narrowly define those fields. That promotes competency in the conservative sense and would have reinforced those skills in the most direct sense.

However, I consider myself fortunate that I was "outside the box" long enough to learn something that was practical and useful in the truest sense of the martial arts. As I am suggesting here, we can all benefit by going outside the margins a little to help our primary fields of interest. And when we do, the public can see our sense of genuine curiosity and cooperation as we interact with other martial artists and our image will be enhanced.

It is wonderful and rewarding to devote the largest percentage of our energies and attention to our primary competency and reap the fruit of that hard work and study. But we should leave room to explore the unknown and unfamiliar as well. That type of openness becomes contagious and reflects well on us.

CHAPTER ELEVEN

WHY MARTIAL ARTS ARE THE BEST EXERCISE

"He who has a 'why' to live for can bear almost any 'how.'"
—NIETZSCHE

Open any Yellow Pages advertising the martial arts and you're sure to see a familiar theme of benefits explaining why someone should begin lessons: confidence, coordination, and self-discipline. This touches on the values previously discussed and are certainly desirable results of our training. However, they don't fully express the reason why martial arts are the best exercise. I think we have "bragging rights" and should be proud of both our heritage and extensive community.

There is some very thoughtful discussion about whether martial arts are in fact an art or a sport.[1] For the moment, set aside whether the martial arts are either one exclusively. To speak a universal language, let's consider ourselves a "sport" for the sake of comparison to similar types of exercise activities. As we do, we discover some compelling reasons why martial arts are the best exercise. These initial reasons include the fact that everyone is welcome, it's practical, and diversity is emphasized.

Everyone is Welcome

There is a familiar adage in Olympic training circles that says "To become an

We are the best sport as we take our licks and keep on smiling.

Olympic athlete, you must choose your parents well." As discussed in Chapter Five, sport scientists and human performance research have demonstrated that genetics, or what you're born with, play a primary role in elite athletic success.

For example, if you're in the mid-five foot range, you can't reasonably expect to be guarding someone like Scottie Pippen of the Chicago Bulls. Height is a "discriminating" factor. Superior endurance athletes (e.g., runners, cyclists, and swimmers) are successful in part due to that (high) inherited "VO_2 Max." Again, this is a "discriminating" factor. But the martial arts don't require you to be a certain height or possess certain characteristics that are only trainable in a limited range (such as the VO_2 Max). Outside the elite or professional context, people of all sizes, lengths, and shapes are welcome.

In fact, martial arts are unique in that intensive training can make up for a lack of inherited ability. Furthermore, our sport accommodates people by dividing competition into categories such as age, weight, and proficiency (i.e., belt levels). Don't you think NFL quarterbacks would like to limit the size of defensive lineman to perhaps 200 pounds? That would make things quite a bit easier for them. Essentially, we do that in the martial arts by competing against others of similar age, weight, and proficiency. The genetics (and training) that may cause someone to be a 300 pound mountain of terror will not be (mandatorily) pitted against a 150 pound junior in high school. The martial arts say "everyone is welcome" by accommodating people of all physical types. This is one reason why our sport is the best.

Someone could say, "there are formal types of amateur athletics in other sports as well like flag football, city basketball leagues, and the like." As a point of argument, there is some truth to that assertion. But do they categorize competition by age, weight, or skill to promote equal opportunity and reduce the threat of injury? No, they don't.

A Practical Exercise

Runners often boast of possessing the most "portable" exercise. As an example, when runners travel on business or pleasure, they only have to carry a pair of running shoes and minimal clothing. No worries about equipment or finding a gym. Thus, the "portable" description. However, some of these runners find there are still obstacles to their exercise while away from home. Their hotel may be in a dangerous part of town where running is unsafe. Or, the weather may be perilous—forcing them inside.

With the martial artist, these considerations are not an obstacle. If a hotel or dormitory room is as far as a person can go for uncontrollable reasons, the martial athlete has many options: stretching, isometrics (e.g., push-ups), *kata*, or any number of activities that can be performed in as little as a space of 8' x 8'. This makes the martial arts even more portable and, in this sense, the most practical athletic endeavor.

Furthermore, as opposed to more one-dimensional sports, the martial arts can be practiced indoors or out and is not dependent on the weather (no rain-outs!). In effect, we are not dependent on circumstances beyond our control—which is very liberating. Moreover, while numerous sports require at least one other person (if not a whole team), we can practice individually or as part of a group. In our sport, there is no disappointment because a tennis partner doesn't show up. Even if we desire to work out with someone who is unable to meet us after all, there is an alternative—we work out by ourselves and our exercise is not necessarily compromised. Again, this makes us more liberated than many sports which are dependent on favorable circumstances or people that are outside individual control. This portability and practicality suggests the inherent superiority of the martial arts.

As with any sport, there are numerous ways to spend a lot of money in the martial arts. Training devices, tournament fees, and seminars are but a few of the alternatives. But at the essential core of martial arts, it can cost absolutely nothing. It is entirely possible to practice the martial arts without spending a dime. While certain equipment and devices certainly enhance training, they are not a mandatory requirement for the martial athlete. A martial artist can exercise in normal clothing and find instruction in books at the public library. I'm not recommending this "spartan" approach for your training (it can be maximized by spending money appropriately). But it does demonstrate that the martial arts are the least expensive of any sport, including running, which at least requires shoes (we don't need them!).

The martial arts are also "less expensive" in some non-monetary ways. For instance, consider injury management. If you're a football player and break a leg, that's a season-ending "costly" experience. Players of many sports feel a sense of futility when their season is ended by an injury. But due to the "range" of the martial arts, there are numerous alternatives during an injury. When I tore a ligament, I certainly didn't spar for a while. But I still hit the heavy bag (sitting down), worked the *nunchakus,* and focused on abdominal training.

Most people are familiar with the Bill Wallace story where due to an injury of his right leg he exclusively used his left during his recovery and developed the trademark "Superfoot" style. We are not "out for the season" as martial artists. That is the type of range and resourcefulness unique to the martial arts. We are, in fact, the most practical and resourceful of all sports because injury to one body part does not stop our training. We train other portions. "When you are ill, you can consider it a heaven-granted rest and use the wonderful opportunity you have for training your spirit."[2] Other sports can't be viewed as positively because they exclusively rely on the physical practice rather than spiritual development as in the martial arts.

Diversity

An emerging emphasis in our society is to recognize diversity. This means to respect other people regardless of their color, religion, or various other social preferences. Many sports are arguably "equal opportunity employers" and feature players of differing races. But when you think about it, the martial arts are probably the most sensitive to racial and cultural diversity than any other sport.

One reason for this appreciation of diversity is the Asian origin of the martial arts. As Americans, we are honoring and recognizing an activity born in another culture. If you've ever been in a training session with a transplanted Korean or Japanese instructor, you know what diversity is all about! The commands require full attention or you will quickly fall behind.

Martial athletes also practice diversity through service, humility, and fierce competition because every training hall has martial athletes of junior rank, those more advanced, and those who are of a similar belt level. This creates an

Diversity also includes reaching out to hearing-impaired martial artists.

interesting interaction amoung martial athletes and is yet another form of diversity. Whereas the competitors of some sports are only interested in what makes them individually excel, the different belt levels present in a training session mean there is always someone to teach (service), someone to be taught by (humility), and someone to gauge our progress against (fierce competition). This range of experience trains our attitudes to accommodate physical, as well as cultural, diversity.

We are all familiar with the Yellow Pages benefits ascribed to the martial arts. Physically, practice promotes strength, muscle tone, flexibility, lower blood pressure, and, of course, self-defense. Because our training is rigorous, we burn more fat calories than lower intensity forms of exercise such as aerobics. Mentally, practice and competition fosters more focus, the ability to deal with pressure, and orients us to achieving both short and long-term goals. But as I alluded to earlier, these can be arguably ascribed to any physically active sport.

The martial arts are simply the best sport because they offer these common benefits while delivering other unique features when compared to other sports. In our sport, you won't be told you're too short or don't have enough money. Instead, a short person will be shown how something like judo is probably a good fit (due to a lower center of gravity). Those without a lot of money can be directed to a local YMCA. And a "rookie" will be shown how to improve his or her techniques so that the junior student eventually achieves expertise and advanced rank.

Even if Martial Art is Only Performed as Sport . . .

As I alluded to at the beginning of this chapter, there is some disagreement about whether martial arts are in fact an art or sport. Some would even say that the sport aspect of martial arts represents compromise, commercialism, and threatens the integrity of the martial arts. In particular, karate point fighting is seen as "unrealistic" and argued to be without value because it doesn't prepare someone for the "street." I question that reasoning.

Let's consider boxing for the moment. Mike Tyson certainly can hit hard in the ring but in the only street fight he's had since becoming a professional he broke his hand on the first punch. Thus, is boxing training for "real life"? Or, how about someone who trains exclusively for "the street" and never engages in a self-defense situation? Was that training wasted? What we really find is that derivatives of martial arts—like karate point fighting—can help prepare martial artists for life in general while providing some indirect benefits such as self-defense and physical conditioning. In the remainder of this chapter, I'll examine how point fighting helps prepare us for life in general—which further suggests martial arts are the best exercise.

Let's begin with the assertion that point fighting is without value. This raises three considerations. First, what is true self-defense training? Second, are there benefits to practicing what may not necessarily save our life? And third, can an activity evolve from it's original intention and still be considered valid? Let's look at all three questions more closely.

True Self-defense

To defend yourself in unarmed combat requires the ability to fight in any conditions at any time against any number or size of opponents. In today's terms, that could mean in a parking lot, on the beach, or perhaps at an athletic stadium. If you're a female, that could mean deflecting male aggression while seated in a car or on a couch.

In other words, if someone claims to only train for "streetwise self-defense," then their training should be in those types of situations. If we only practiced martial arts for pure self-defense, we probably wouldn't even have *dojos*. We would be in the locations that resemble our daily lives and our training uniforms wouldn't be *gis* but our everyday clothes. And, we'd be wearing shoes, not training barefoot.

Even those who reject karate point fighting train in conditions that are not, by definition, oriented for the street (in it's strictest terms). The techniques may be more forceful than the deliberately restrained movements used to score points in a tournament, but the "true self-defense" application is blunted by practice in (martial art) clothing and conditions that don't reflect daily life.

Train According to Your Objective

Instead of accepting the abstract arguments about what best prepares you for the street, the lesson here is to practice for the result you individually desire. If you want "true self-defense," then ask your instructor and peers to meet you at your school, work, or neighborhood to train in the conditions where you might actually have to defend yourself.

On the other hand, if your objective is broader, such as the sport aspect or development of character available through karate point fighting, then pursue that goal with a clean conscience. Admittedly, you won't learn as much about self-defense by scoring a point with a reverse punch as you would by learning joint locks. But point fighting has many benefits as one of the many expressions of the martial arts.

Point Fighting Benefits

There are both physical and psychological gains to be considered. Physically, point fighting teaches you how to determine your fighting distance (how close you need to be to your opponent to score). This can be applied to the street as well. Point fighting also teaches you how to avoid being hit, which seems like a very desirable trait for fighting in the street. Thus, you not only learn how close you have to be to score a point, you also learn how far to stay back to avoid being hit.

Another great benefit to point fighting is learning appropriate degrees of aggression. You simply can't execute every technique like your life depends on it. If you did, both you and your opponent would be unduly injured or outright dead! Do football players hit as hard during the week as on Sunday? Of course not. They would wear themselves out. In the same way, point fighting allows you to learn how to pull techniques and control your aggression so that it can be used in greater degrees when necessary.

Another consideration is that point fighting tends to induce greater degrees of physical conditioning than only training for streetwise self-defense. In my observations over the past couple of decades, I have noted numerous instructors die before age 60 of heart failure (some before age 50!). In most cases, these were people who did not exercise as rigorously as they should.

Point fighting teaches us how to determine distance.

Instead of training to compete (which induces physical conditioning), they were perfecting throws and other forms of techniques that did not adequately exercise their cardiovascular systems.

Psychological Benefits

Some of the people who reject karate point fighting as a martial art do so because they believe the sport aspect erodes the goals for developing martial art character (i.e., the "Martial Way"). In particular, there is a concern about an undue emphasis on winning. But that's actually one of the primary psychological benefits of point fighting.

In the tournament atmosphere we are challenged to both win, and lose, graciously. Just as certain professional football games are decided by the subjective calls of a referee, so our "win" in point fighting may be either deserved or undeserved (depending on the referees). That has a specific application to life in general as many outcomes will be decided beyond our control in work

> **Learning to "live" with the decision of a referee, whether correct or not, helps build emotional maturity that can be used outside the competitive arena.**

and relationships. Thus, learning to "live" with the decision of a referee, whether correct or not, helps build emotional maturity that can be used outside the competitive arena.

Still, some would say the subjective nature of competing is just too unfair. But that is exactly what can inspire us to win and lose with a high degree of character. Because we may win today and lose tomorrow, we learn to treat our opponent, and ourselves, with a fundamental respect that is not tied to results. When we win, that's great. When we "lose," we have an opportunity to learn something about ourselves and our techniques. This is consistent with the Martial Way.

Karate point fighting also enables us to confront our fears, which is another specific application to life in general. The proponents of exclusive training for streetwise self-defense may practice endlessly before using those techniques in a "real life" situation (as in decades). In turn, even the most refined techniques may be useless if sudden, unexpected fear is experienced the first time those techniques must actually be used.

In contrast, point fighting allows us to learn about our fears on a continual basis. Sometimes we fear losing and feel the rush of adrenaline just before the match. Due to point fighting, we learn to manage that anxiety. At other times, we fear an opponent because of his or her greater size only to discover they were pushovers. We might also underestimate someone because of their smaller size only to find ourselves on the losing end. Point fighting allows us to experience our fears, now, as well as our prejudices. This is consistent with the martial Way.

A third psychological benefit to karate point fighting is the skill of goal setting. Due to the tournament schedule, we learn to set goals and train due to our anticipated competition. This is a great catalyst for training and physical conditioning—knowing we have an event in the foreseeable future. In turn, we learn to say "no" to things that don't complement our goal and say "yes" to the things that do. What we avoid will probably include things that are adverse

Point fighting encourages arduous training we might not otherwise pursue.

for our health. This, too, increases the quality of our lives and contributes to the martial arts as the best sport.

Intention vs. Evolution

I also noted a third consideration in assessing the value of karate point fighting. Detractors state that it is useless because it doesn't relate to true self-defense, which is the original intention of the martial arts. I agree that the relationship of point fighting to many self-defense situations is arguably indirect. But as we saw in the discussion of the benefits, there are numerous advantages to karate point fighting that are reflective of the overall goal of the martial arts.

What is more pressing is whether we as the martial arts community will recognize the evolution of our art's original intention. In other words, when the martial arts spawn off new activities, such as karate point fighting (a 20th century innovation), what is our proper response?

First of all, we must accept evolution. The U.S. Constitution is amended to integrate changing needs. If we didn't allow change from original intention then we wouldn't have our broad voting rights or the Civil Rights Act. In a

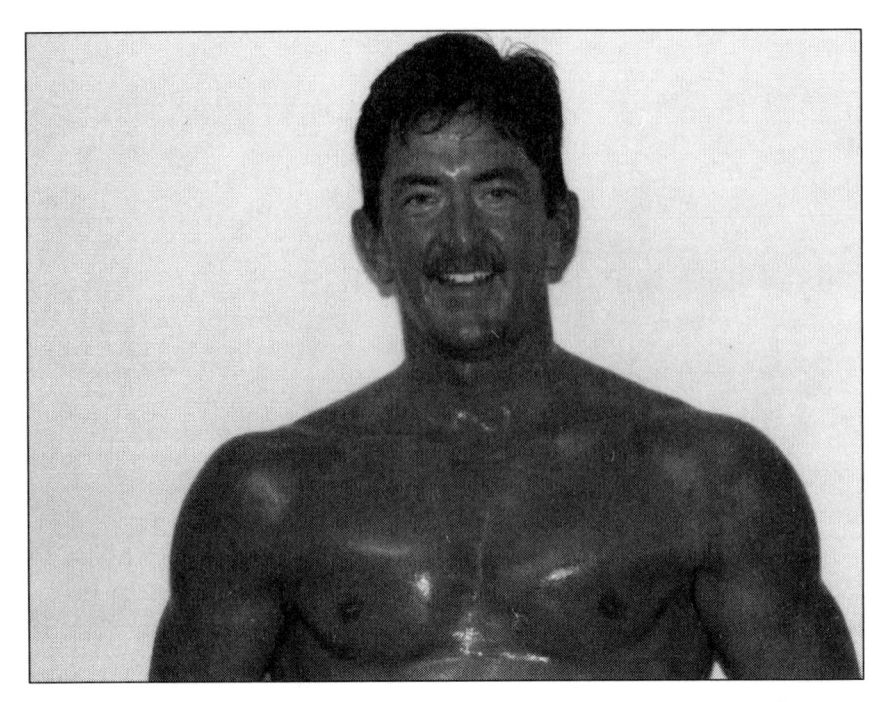

The author has found the martial arts to welcome everyone, promote diversity, and be the most practical of all exercises

sport example, did you know that the forward pass was originally illegal in football? Can you imagine the game without it today? Just because our activities don't precisely match the original intention doesn't invalidate the evolutionary aspect.

Secondly, the true worth of any activity is measured against its individual objective. Karate point fighting may not fully prepare you for a parking lot situation, but neither does training barefoot or learning to throw opponents in a judo uniform (which won't tear like normal cotton garments you would encounter on the street). As Daeshik Kim has observed, without having experience in different martial arts, you cannot be objective about what is valuable in a single martial art. Karate point fighting is an experience of the martial arts that both draw people into practice initially and serve as an introduction to discovering other segments of the martial arts overall. As a community, therefore, let's reinforce the positive aspects of karate point fighting to realize what is worthy about all martial arts.

We are the best!

CLOSING THOUGHTS

What we really need as martial artists is a total existence. We must integrate our training, work, and relationships into a comprehensive quality effort. Throughout this book, I have outlined principles that will empower your Total Quality endeavor. I have demonstrated that this means incorporating a lot of variables: sport science and systematic training for your athletic performance; true spirituality for your work and relationships; a sense of service with regard to the martial arts community and public perception.

To the extent that I have been successful in these efforts, I thank the Lord Jesus Christ for providing the motivation and giving me the resolve to persevere.

The Total Quality approach outlined in this book is both simple and complex at the same time. Technically stated, it means committing to the discipline of recording your life in a journal or in comparative logs. This means your athletic performance as well as your personal life. Has your mother ever given you a letter that you wrote at a younger age that you tried to disavow? We shirk from those things because the truth, which is often our immaturity and generalized thinking patterns, hurts! We don't like to be accountable by writing things down in order to compare our progress. It can be humbling.

But the discipline of "journaling" is what will make the principles outlined in this book flourish for you. By recording what I do, I know that heart-rate based, systematic training revolutionized my athletic life. By maintaining a personal journal, I see the undesirable behavioral patterns that I have created throughout the years that I now want to break.

The Total Quality Martial Arts approach means just what the title implies: Total Quality efforts and results in all that we do. It does not mean that we must finish ahead of someone else. But it does mean that our results must reflect our most intelligent, sincere, and intense efforts. Research it, experience it, record it, compare it, experience it again. That is the process of Total Quality. These principles can be applied to every aspect of your life.

I believe there is that aspect of human laziness in us all that sees growth in particular areas become stagnant through neglect. If we repress or neglect one part of ourselves, it will eventually overthrow our personal lives.[3] Thus, if we're fitness enthusiasts (fanatics), our relationships or work may suffer. If we're more extroverted, our fitness goals may suffer. That is why the principle of accountability is so important. You need logs or other written forms that record your various activities and a strong mentor in order to embrace accountability. Without it, your best friend might be someone named "mediocrity."

I sincerely hope that Part Two on spiritual growth is helpful to you. How many times have I seen myself or someone else think that achieving athletic performance would solve their problems? When work is boring or a relationship is strained, we amateur athletes look at the faces of those who win and think that winning must be what we need to be "well." That simply is not true. The torn lives of the professional athletes previously mentioned show us that. The work that we are doing on this planet is to get present[4] in all areas of our lives.

So, let us be successful martial artists of the worthwhile kind: well-trained, successful in our work and relationships, and with an eye to the future. That is Total Quality Martial Arts.

REFERENCES

PART ONE

Introduction

1. Carr, David; Littman, Ian (1990). *Excellence in Government: Total Quality Management in the 1990s.* Arlington, VA: Coopers & Lybrand. (p. 21)

2. Friman, Richard H. (1996). "Blinded by the Light: Politics and Profit in the Martial Arts." *Journal of Asian Martial Arts,* 5 (3), pp. 11–19.

Chapter One

1. Hatfield, Fredrick C. (1993). *Fitness: The Complete Guide.* Santa Barbara, CA: International Sport Sciences Association. (p. 102).

2. Staley, Charles I. (1996). *Special Topics in Martial Arts Conditioning.* Santa Barbara, CA: Myo-Dynamics. (p. 70)

3. Lee, Bruce (1975). *Tao of Jeet Kune Do.* Burbank, CA: Ohara. (p. 46)

4. Morgan, Forrest E. (1992). *Living the Martial Way.* Emeryville, CA: Barricade Books. (pp. 215–16)

5. Ehrhard, Tom (1994, February). "The Best Training Plan . . . Period." *Bicycling,* pp. 69–72.

6. Sleamaker, Rob (1989). *Serious Training for Serious Athletes.* Champaign, IL: Leisure Press.

7. Mitchell, David (1988). *The Martial Arts Coaching Manual.* London, England: A&C Black. (p. 24)

Chapter Two

1. Kraemer, William J. (1994). "General Adaptations to Resistance and Endurance Training Programs." In *Essentials of Strength Training and Conditioning.* Champaign, IL: Human Kinetics. (p. 141)

2. Koch, Fred (1995). *Strength Training for Sports.* Oxnard, CA: Applied Futuristics.

3. Storm, Mitch (1986). "Bruce Lee's Training Methods." In *The Legendary Bruce Lee.* Burbank, CA: O'Hara Publications. (p. 53).

4. Janssen, Peter (1987). *Training Lactate Pulserate.* Oulu, Finland: Polar Electro Oy. (p. 19)

5. Jeffrey, Douglas (1996, May). "Supple and Flexible." *MA Training,* pp. 6–12.

6. Wallace, Bill (1982). *Dynamic Stretching and Kicking.* Burbank, CA: Unique Publications.

Chapter Three

1. Editors. (1996, November). "Jeff Speakman." *Black Belt,* p. 165.

2. Ebben, William P. & Blackard, Douglas O. (1997, February). "Developing a Strength-Power Program for Amatuer Boxing." *Strength and Conditioning,* pp. 42–51.

3. Ibid

4. Hatfield, Fredrick C. (1993). *Fitness: The Complete Guide.* Santa Barbara, CA: International Sport Sciences Association. (p. 102)

5. Waldron, Meg (1994, February). "Strength: Determining Muscle Type." *Runner's World,* (p. 34)

6. Volek, Jeff S., Houseknecht, Kent, & Kramer, William J. (1997, February). "Nutritional Strategies to Enhance Performance of High-Intensity Exercise." *Strength and Conditioning.* (pp. 11–17)

7. Potteiger, Jeffrey A. (1997, February). "Dose-Response for Creatine Monohydrate Supplementation." *Strength and Conditioning.* (p. 23)

8. Sears, Barry (1995). *The Zone.* New York, NY: Harper Collins.

REFERENCES

Chapter Four

1. Lee, Linda (1989). *The Bruce Lee Story.* Burbank, CA: O'hara Publications. (pp. 70–71)

2. Brisacher, Art (1996). *Maximize Your Martial Arts Training: The Martial Arts Training Diary.* Wethersfield, CT: Turtle Press. (pp. 142–45)

3. Egami, Shigeru (1976). *The Heart of Karate-Do.* New York, NY: Harper & Row. (p. 15)

4. Tohei, Koichi (1966). *Aikido in Daily Life.* Tokyo, Japan: Rikugei Publishing House. (pp. 164–65)

5. Jackson, Phil & Delehanty, Hugh (1995). *Sacred Hoops: Spiritual Lessons of a Hardwood Warrior.* New York, NY: Hyperion. (p. 109)

6. Meyer, Ron & Stone, John (1995). *Aikido in America.* Berkeley, CA: Frog, Ltd. (p. 232)

7. Gummerson, Tony (1992). *Training Theory for Martial Arts.* London, England: A&C Black. (pp. 86–109)

8. Young, Robert W. (1996, October). "Karate Cops: Civilian Martial Arts Advisory Panel for the LAPD." *Karate/Kung-Fu Illustrated,* pp. 68–69.

9. Carradine, David (1991). *The Spirit of Shaolin.* Boston, MA: Tuttle Publishing (p. 110)

PART TWO

Introduction

1. Kauz, Herman (1992). *A Path to Liberation.* Woodstock, NY: Overlook Press. (pp. 73–74)

2. Peck, M. Scott. (1978). *The Road Less Traveled.* New York, NY: Simon and Schuster.

3. Ibid. (p. 107).

4. Kim, Daeshik (1987). *Background Readings in TaeKwonDo and Martial Arts.* Seoul, Korea: NANAM Publications. (p. 38)

5. Salzman, Mark (1995). *Lost in Place.* New York, NY: Vintage Press. (p. 11)

6. Hassell, Randall G. (1980). *The Karate Experience: a Way of Life.* Boston, MA: Tuttle Publishing. (p. 34)

7. Coleman, Jim. (1997, March). "Van Damme Enters Substance Abuse Clinic." *Black Belt*, p. 10.

8. Maliszewski, Michael (1996). *Spiritual Dimensions of the Martial Arts.* Boston, MA: Tuttle Publishing. (p. 131)

9. Covey, Stephen (1989). *The Seven Habits of Highly Effective People.* New York, NY: Simon and Schuster.

Chapter Five

1. Niednagel, Jonathan P. (1992). *Your Best Sport: How to Choose and Play It.* Laguna Niguel, CA: Laguna Press. (pp. 150–52)

2. Tiidus, Peter M. & Zabukovec, Randy (1995, November). "Physiological and Anthropometric Profile of Elite Kickboxers." *Journal of Strength and Conditioning Research,* pp. 240–42.

3. Sheehan, George (1992). *George Sheehan on Running to Win.* Emmaus, PA: Rodale Press. (p. 35)

4. Noakes, Timothy (1991). *The Lore of Running.* Champaign, IL: Leisure Press. (p. 23)

Chapter Six

1. Beck, Charlotte Joko (1993). *Nothing Special: Living Zen.* San Francisco, CA: Harper & Row. (p. 63)

2. Kauz, Herman (1992). *A Path to Liberation.* Woodstock, NY: Overlook Press. (pp. 73–74)

3. Watts, Alan (1957). *The Way of Zen.* New York, NY: Vintage Press. (p. 146)

4. Hobain, Jack (1988) *Ninpo: Living and Thinking as a Warrior.* Chicago, IL: Contemporary Books. (pp. 43–44)

5. Deshimaru, Taisen (1982). *The Zen Way to the Martial Arts.* New York, NY: E. P. Dutton. (p. 54)

6. Samuels, Allison & Leland, John (1997, March 17). "Hard to the Hoop." *Newsweek.*

7. Sinetar, Marsha (1992). *Work as a Spiritual Path.* Boulder, CO: Sounds True Productions.

8. Beck, Charlotte Joko (1993). *Nothing Special: Living Zen.* San Francisco, CA: Harper & Row.

REFERENCES

9. Beck, Charlotte Joko (1989). *Everyday Zen.* San Francisco, CA: Harper & Row.

Chapter Seven

1. Funakoshi, Gichin (1975). *Karate-Do: My Way of Life.* Tokyo, Japan: Kodansha International. (p. 102)

2. Palmer, Wendy (1994). *The Intuitive Body: Aikido as a Clairsentient Practice.* Berkeley, CA: North Atlantic Books.

3. Tohei, Koichi (1966). *Aikido in Daily Life.* Tokyo, Japan: Rikugei Publishing House. (p. 149)

4. Norris, Chuck (1996). *The Secret Power Within: Zen Solutions to Real Problems.* Boston, MA: Little, Brown & Co. (p. 41)

5. Hyams, Joe (1979). *Zen in the Martial Arts.* New York, NY: Bantam. (p. 67)

6. Covey, Stephen (1989). *The Seven Habits of Highly Effective People.* New York, NY: Simon and Schuster.

7. Senge, Peter M. (1990). *The Fifth Discipline.* New York, NY: Doubleday.

8. Bradshaw, John (1992). *Creating Love: The Next Great Stage of Growth.* New York, NY: Bantam.

PART THREE

Chapter Eight

1. Shim, Sang Kyu (1980). *The Making of a Martial Artist.* Detroit, MI: The Author.

2. Mick, Sean (1997, March). "Bruce Lee, the Teacher." *Black Belt,* p. 18.

3. Norris, Chuck; Hyams, Joe (1988). *The Secret of Inner Strength: My Story.* New York, NY: Charter. (p. 226)

4. Friel, Joe (1996). *The Cyclist's Training Bible.* Boulder, CO: Velo Press. (pp. 52–53)

5. Durst, Michael G. (1988). *Napkin Notes: On the Art of Living.* Evanston, IL: Training Systems, Inc. (p. 49)

6. Ibid. (p. 74)

7. Ibid. (p. 72)

8. Robbins, Anthony (1986). *Unlimited Power.* New York, NY: Ballantine.

9. Robbins, Anthony (1991). *Awaken the Giant Within.* New York, NY: Simon and Schuster.

10. Ibid. (p. 42)

Chapter Nine

1. Haines, Bruce a. (1968). *Karate's History and Traditions.* Boston, MA: Tuttle Publishing. (p. 161)

2. Friman, Richard H. (1996). "Blinded by the Light: Politics and Profit in the Martial Arts." *Journal of Asian Martial Arts,* 5 (3), pp. 11–19.

3. Ibid.

4. Jeffrey, Douglas (1996, Fall). "Judo Instructor of the Year: Mike Swain." *Black Belt Yearbook,* pp. 48–49.

5. Levit, Theodore (1975, Sept./Oct.). "Marketing Myopia." *Harvard Business Review,* pp. 26–48.

6. Boudreau, Francoise, Folman, Ralph, & Konzak, Burt (1995). "Parental Observations: Psychological and Physical Changes in School-age Karate Participants." *Journal of Asian Martial Arts,* 4 (4), pp. 50–69.

7. DePasquale, Michael Jr. (1996, Oct./Nov.). "America Online." *Karate International,* p. 39.

8. Goodson, Wilson (1996, October). "Let Your Fingers Do the Browsing." *Inside Kung-Fu,* pp. 48–49

9. Wakai, Sandra (1996, October). "The World Wide What?" *Inside Kung-Fu,* pp. 49, 76, 92.

10. Tucker, Rich (1996, June). "Sprint Training for the Information Highway." *Strength and Conditioning,* pp. 68–71.

11. Jackson, Phil & Delehanty, Hugh (1995). *Sacred Hoops: Spiritual Lessons of a Hardwood Warrior.* New York, NY: Hyperion. (p. 102)

12. Editors. (1991, July). *Introduction to Indoor Air Quality.* EPA publication, 400/3-91/002.

Chapter Ten

1. Editor. (1996, July 12). "Toughman Contests Banned." *The Kansas City Star.*

2. Hess, Christopher D. (1990). "Targeting New Markets for the Martial Arts." Masters Thesis: Webster University, Kansas City, Missouri.

3. Editor. (1996, July 12). "U.S. Needs to Shape Up, Report Says." *Kansas City Star,* pp. A–5.

4. Editor. (1996, August). "Study Proves Tai-Chi Helps Frail Elderly." *Martial Arts Professional,* p 7.) Supplemental information from National Public Radio broadcasts.)

5. Kim, Chong W., Trulson, Michael E. & Padgett, Vernon R. (1985, January). "That Mild-Mannered Bruce Lee." *Psychology Today,* p. 79.

6. Smith, Robert A. (1972). *A Social History of the Bicycle.* New York, NY: American Heritage Press.

7. Friman, Richard H. (1996). "Blinded by the Light: Politics and Profit in the Martial Arts" *Journal of Asian Martial Arts, 5* (3), pp. 11–19.

8. Urban, Peter (1967). *The Karate Dojo: Traditions and Tales of a Martial Art.* Boston, MA: Tuttle Publishing. (pp. 142–145)

9. Ibid

10. Friman, Richard H. (1996). "Blinded by the Light: Politics and Profit in the Martial Arts" *Journal of Asian Martial Arts, 5* (3), pp. 11–19.

11. Oyama, Mas (1978). *Mas Oyama's Essential Karate.* New York, NY: Sterling Publishing (p. 246)

Chapter Eleven

1. Kim, Daeshik, Dr. & Back, Allan (1989). *Martial Meditation: Philosophy and the Essence of the Martial Arts.* Akron, OH: The International Council on Martial Arts Education Press. (pp. 58–88)

2. Tohei, Koichi (1966). *Aikido in Daily Life.* Tokyo, Japan: Rikugei Publishing House. (p. 106)

3. Mindell, Arnold (1992). *The Leader as Martial Artist.* San Francisco, CA: Harper. (p. 7)

4. Siegel, Andrea (1993). *Women in Aikido.* Berkley, CA: North Atlantic Books.

APPENDIX

International Sport Science Association

> 1035 Santa Barbara Street, Suite 7
> Santa Barbara, CA 93101
> ATTN: Charles Staley
> 800-892-4772; FAX 805-884-8119

National Strength and Conditioning Association

> P.O. Box 38909
> Colorado Springs, CO 80937-8909
> 719-632-6722; FAX 719-632-6367

Software for Designing Training Programs

> "MaxPerformer for Coaches." Performance Software Systems. 800-397-3332.

> "Training Design" (Version 6.1). M-F Athletic Company. P.O. Box 8090, Cranston, RI 02920-0090. 800-556-7464

Temperament Assessment

> Association for Psychological Type, 9140 Ward Parkway, Kansas City, Missouri, 64114; 816-444-3500

> Jon Niednagel, Type Dynamics, P.O. Box 6171, Laguna Niguel, CA, 92677; 714-495-6313

INDEX

Author's history, xiii, 92
Absorption (passive recovery), 45-48
Advocacy, 180-184
Cadre training, 169
Comparative Performance Indicators, 73
Creatine monohydrate, 61-64
Decentralization, challenge to martial arts, 186-188
Diversity, 191-193, 195-196
Elite athletes, 97-98
    Use of training programs, 8, 79-80
Endurance training
    Effects on high energy systems, 10
Energy systems, 11-12
    Muscle fiber type application and, 15-19
F.B.I. (author's application process), 134-136
Funakoshi, Gichin, 122

Glycogen (carbohydrates), 57
Growth, perspective on numerical, 176-177
Heart rate (calculating), 36

Insulin, role in performance, 66-68
L.A.P.D., use of Total Quality process, 79
Lifeplanning, 41
    Visioning, 143-144
    Objectives, 145
    Strategies and Tiers, 145-148
Love (defined), 127
Marketing (defined), 160-162
Martial art as sport, 196-202
Mental potential, 150
    Assessment profile, 151-153
    Characterisics of elite athletes, 93-96
    Myers-Briggs Type Indicator, 93-94
Muscle fiber types, 13-14, 54, 100-102
Nutrition, 55-68
    Strategies, 58-63
Periodization, 20-23
Point fighting, benefits, 198-200
Population, U.S. estimate of martial art, 159
Potential (determining), 91
    In cardiovascular fitness, 99-100
    In muscle fiber type, 100-102

In temperment, 93-96
Powerlessness, personal feeling of, 153-154
Practicality (of martial art exercise), 193-194
Public perception (of martial arts), 179
Relationships
   Advice for improving, 129
   As part of Total Quality emphasis, 128
   Communication steps, 130-132
   Inhibitors, 127
Self-beliefs, 155-156
Spirituality, perspectives
   Definition, 85
   Herman Kauz, 85
   Scott Peck, 85-86
Sport science, 171
   Effects of indoor air, 172-176
Strength training, 49-55
   Size expectations, 53-54
Technology, role in Martial Art future, 166-168
Total Quality Management (TQM), history of, x
Total Quality Performance Log, 69, 72-79

Training logs, 77-78
Training plans
   Analysis of results, 74-76
   Benefits of, 26
   Determining volume, 28
   "In the margins", 42-44
   Macro-, Meso-, Microcycles, 23, 29, 30-31
   Martial Art components, 33-40
   Specificity in selection, 13
Unworthiness, personal feeling of, 154
Values, marketing
   Primary, 162,164
   Secondary, 163
Vocation, 107
   Alternatives, 114, 118-120
   As spiritual matter, 108-109
   Assessments for placement, 111
   Dissatisfaction in, 112
Winning, perspectives on, 125
   Phil Jackson, 71
   George Leonard, 71-72
   Kochi Tohei, 70
"Zone" (Dr. Sears approach), 64-66

PHOTO CREDITS

Dennis Cage: pages xii, 11, 27, 57, 60, 67, 75, 95, 110, 122, 161, 174, 192, 195, 199.

Christopher D. Hess: pages 9, 16, 33, 34, 37, 38, 50, 61, 86, 97, 118, 142, 155, 162, 166, 172, 201.

Hannah B. Hess: pages xiv, 4, 6, 18, 54, 62, 202.

Wayne Kaiser: pages xv, 48, 181.